Country Fair
Food & Crafts

Food Editor: Sheryle Eastwood
Craft Editor: Tonia Todman
Assistant Food Editor: Rachel Blackmore
Assistant Craft Editors: Judy Poulos, Sally Pereira
Editorial Coordinator: Margaret Kelly
Editorial Assistant: Marian Broderick
Text: Vicky Fraser, Denise Greig and Judy Poulos
Craft Assistance: Kate Fury, Carol Todman, Cecily
Rogers, Elsie Hamerlok, Sophie Levitt, Sue Leech,
Louise Pfanner

Photography: Andrew Elton
Styling: Michelle Gorry

DESIGN AND PRODUCTION
Production Managers: Sheridan Carter,
Anna Maguire
Production Coordinator: Meredith Johnston
Layout and Finished Art: Monica Kessler-Tay,
Barbara Martusewicz, Chris Hatcher

Published by J. B. Fairfax Press Pty Limited
80-82 McLachlan Avenue
Rushcutters Bay, NSW 2011, Australia

Formatted by J. B. Fairfax Press Pty Limited
Output by Adtype, Sydney
Printed by Toppan Printing Co., Singapore

©J. B. Fairfax Press Pty Limited, 1990
This book is copyright. No part may be reproduced
or transmitted without the written permission of the
publisher. Enquiries should be made in writing to
the publisher.

JBFP 9 R2
Includes index
ISBN 1 86343 002 4

DISTRIBUTION AND SALES
J. B. Fairfax Press Pty Limited
Ph: (02) 9361 6366 Fax: (02) 9360 6262
http://www.jbfp.com.au

Contents

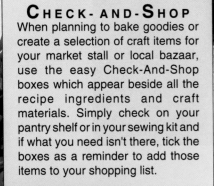

CHECK-AND-SHOP

When planning to bake goodies or create a selection of craft items for your market stall or local bazaar, use the easy Check-And-Shop boxes which appear beside all the recipe ingredients and craft materials. Simply check on your pantry shelf or in your sewing kit and if what you need isn't there, tick the boxes as a reminder to add those items to your shopping list.

Introduction

Fetes, fairs and bazaars go back a long way – beyond childhood memories of sweet sticky toffees, hooplas and candy floss. For centuries such festivities have brought us together to celebrate fine food, crafts, lively entertainment and great bargains. Today's fetes, fairs and markets still retain that wonderful sense of excitement and, whether they are cosy get-togethers at the local kindergarten, the annual church bazaar or full-scale extravaganzas, they usually offer a fantastic selection of beautiful handicrafts and delicious home-made sweets and savouries. These days, they are not only festive and fun occasions but also major fundraising events. Now if it's your turn to go behind the scenes and make it all happen, don't be daunted. Organising a fete can be lots of fun and very rewarding as well as raising much-needed funds for your school or church group.

SAFETY NOTE: If you are making toys for your local bazaar or fete, make sure you use safety eyes and noses. Buttons, bows and other loose trimmings, should not be used if toys are for babies or very small children. All toys made for resale must comply with new E.C. Regulations.

How to plan for profit

Organising a fundraising fete or bazaar takes time – from three months to a year. The real key to success is an active and inspired committee who will in turn activate the rest of the group to contribute their skill and labour!

Each stall should have its own committee, made up of a convener, secretary and treasurer and as many members as needed to make a comfortable working group. The committee has overall responsibility for making or collecting the goods for sale, seeking donations of raw materials or prizes and setting up and running the stall on the day. Ideally, the committee will organise fundraising social events in the month prior to the fete. The money raised can be used to finance their stall without needing to make too many further demands for funds.

It is essential to have a team of reliable, eager volunteers. Enlist the help of as many people as you can, especially those with the special talents you require for your stall. Make certain that all volunteers are welcomed and suitable jobs found for them all.

Let each person determine how much work they are willing to do. If lots of things need to be made, consider supplying your helpers with some or all of the raw materials so the cost does not deter people from helping.

Meetings go hand in hand with committees and need not be boring, dragged out affairs. If they are run in a relaxed, informal way, a meeting can be lots of fun and a great way to get people involved and busy.

Regular meetings are important for planning, allocating tasks and reviewing progress, and also provide great opportunities for sharing ideas and skills. Take careful notes.

THE COUNTDOWN

With such a variety of tasks to be completed over several months, a countdown calendar is an excellent way of checking the progress of various elements. This is especially crucial for craft items and other goods that are time consuming to make or may need to mature, such as plants and relishes. To draw up a countdown calendar:

❖ Start with the big date, work backwards, plotting the completion dates for each stage of the preparation program.
❖ Be a little flexible, allowing extra time for the unexpected as very rarely do things go exactly as planned.

Left: Beautiful embroidery as a fundraiser

Top right: Well-packaged gourmet treats

❖ Review your calendar regularly and, if necessary, reassess the dates.

As with all successful ventures, effective organisation will minimise problems and ensure that the buildup to the big day is more fun than frustration.

MONEY, MONEY, MONEY!

The committees need to take a fairly professional approach to money matters whether they are fund-raising, budgeting and setting targets, or handling money on the day. Each stall committee should follow these simple guidelines:

❖ Work out how much money you want to raise. Set a target based on last year's takings with a modest increase added.

❖ Estimate the total costs involved in producing the goods and setting up the stall.

❖ To minimise outlay, aim to have as many materials as possible donated or purchase them at a discount rate.

❖ Don't overlook hidden costs, such as public insurance liability, employment of a security guard or hauling away rubbish afterwards.

❖ If you are selling highly-priced items you may wish to establish credit facilities – if so, apply to the bank early and check the costs involved.

❖ You will need a secure area for holding and counting money on the day. Ideally it will be a room, large enough for three or four people, with a single access which is easily locked.

Pricing is always a thorny problem – generally buyers are looking for bargains, but will be happy to pay a little more for something they specially want.

Before opening for business, make sure each stall has a reasonable amount of change to start off with. Don't allow large amounts of money to be kept at the stall – arrange for two reliable people to collect money from each stall at regular intervals. Hold all collected money in your secure room until it can be counted and banked.

Take into account any outlays when deciding on price and also the possibility that you may have to discount perishable items toward the end of the day. Generally prices should be a little below the local shop prices for similar items but always allowing for a premium for the handmade and unique.

PUBLICITY

No matter how large or small your fete is, the more publicity you generate beforehand, the better attended it will be. Appoint a publicity officer to plan a well-organised campaign using a variety of methods to attract attention to the event.

Look for opportunities for free publicity – announcements on community radio stations and diary dates in local newspapers are good starting points. If you have a particularly newsworthy attraction at the fete or a celebrity to open it, contact the features editor of the newspaper with details.

Local shopkeepers are usually willing to place notices or posters for worthy causes in their windows. Some may even be prepared to hand out leaflets to customers. Why not organise a competition among local youngsters to design a fete poster? There should be a prize for the winner and all the posters, winners and losers alike, should be exhibited. Remind parents of a school fete by sending home notices with the children. Large banners (the larger the better) and coloured bunting are great attention-getters, so make sure they are strategically placed around the venue at least two weeks beforehand.

If you can afford paid publicity, it may be worthwhile investing in advertising in the local press or printing and delivering leaflets around the neighbourhood.

PLANNING THE EVENT

Planning a fundraising event usually begins with setting a date. Choose a day that does not clash with public holidays or other local events. If you need to select and book a venue, do so as early as possible and ask for confirmation in writing.

When deciding what stalls to have, include the traditional attractions such as the cake, sweet, gourmet foods and craft stalls. These are great money spinners and, together with a range of entertainment to suit all ages, will provide a good nucleus. We have included some wonderful fun ideas for stalls and lots of hints on how to run them.

Make sure there is plenty of tempting snack-type food to select from – sausage sizzling barbecue, fruit salad, hamburgers and sandwiches. Provide a quiet, comfortable retreat for harassed parents, friends and organisers to sit down for a Devonshire tea.

Competitions are an excellent attraction, particularly raffles or grand draws, with winners announced on the day. Some of the stalls can organise their own raffles with prizes such as our lovely embroidered cushion. Plan these well in advance and don't forget to check if there are any regulations governing the running of competitions. Approach local businesses for prizes and have any offers confirmed in writing. Ask a local celebrity to present the prizes.

TIMETABLE OF EVENTS

When planning the program for the day don't make it too drawn out. Remember there will be lots of cleaning and packing up to do after closing time and everyone will be tired. As lunchtime is the busiest period of the day, arrange to put on one major event before midday and another in the early afternoon.

It is worthwhile appointing a master of ceremonies to announce forthcoming events over a public address system. If stalls have their own loudspeakers, make sure they don't drown each other out by all speaking at once. A fun way to convey information about coming attractions is to have volunteers dressed as clowns or minstrels wandering through the crowd and spreading the word.

DESIGNING THE LAYOUT

When deciding where to position the stalls, keep in mind which ones require power points, taps or shady positions (such as the cake stall).

Include an area for first aid, lost children and lost property, and

Scented sachets filled with lavender and potpourri

alternative arrangements. Without forward planning all your efforts could be washed down the drain!

STALL PRESENTATION

A friendly appealing stall will be a real attraction. Be as imaginative and creative as you like – it will certainly pay dividends. Consider having a theme which is carried through in the various stalls and entertainments.

Instead of plain trestles or stands, cover them with fabric or paper and use shelving, baskets and the support poles of the stand to display your wares. Colour and fun should be the order of the day!

Packaging is equally important. Make goods irresistible by using lots of cellophane paper, pretty ribbon and decorative price tags.

If you are looking for inspiration, the wealth of creative ideas for stall presentation, packaging and displays to be found throughout this book are guaranteed to set you on the right path.

ON THE DAY

Depending on security and the type of stall, you may be able to set up and at least partially stock some stands the night before. If not, allow plenty of time before the opening and recruit volunteers to help set up and decorate the stall. Don't clutter the display – keep extra stock in boxes under the counter or in a cool place and replenish the stall regularly from these reserves.

Create a roster for those manning the stalls so that everyone has some time off to enjoy themselves. Lunchtime is likely to be one of the busiest times, especially if you are selling food, so roster on extra people during this time. You will also need a team of willing

helpers to clean up and dismantle everything at closing time. Arrange with your local authority for removal of rubbish, of which there is likely to be a great deal, at the end of the day's festivities.

METRIC IMPERIAL	
METRIC	INCHES
2 mm	$^1/_{16}$
6 mm	$^1/_4$
1 cm	$^3/_8$
2.5 cm	1
5 cm	2
30 cm	12
91 cm	36

MEASURING UP	
CUPS	
$^1/_4$ cup	60 mL
$^1/_3$ cup	80 mL
$^1/_2$ cup	125 mL
1 cup	250 mL
SPOONS	
$^1/_4$ teaspoon	1.25 mL
$^1/_2$ teaspoon	2.5 mL
1 teaspoon	5 mL
1 tablespoon	20 mL

Enthusiastic customers at the barbecue.

signpost the toilets clearly. If you are able to provide parking, set aside an area close to the stalls for stallholders so they don't have too far to carry their goods. If your fete covers a large area, place signs to direct people to stands and activities.

The great anxiety of all organisers is waking up on the big day to an overcast sky and the threat of rain. Always have a back-up plan in case of wet weather and make sure everyone is aware of the

Cake stall delights

The cake stall, with its wonderful array of goodies, is always popular and profitable. Few people can withstand the temptation of a beautifully presented selection of home-baked cakes, biscuits and slices.

A wide range of high quality cakes, biscuits and slices is the key to a successful stall.

Divide your baking into categories, such as cakes, biscuits and slices, and draw up a master plan for each. The plan should cover:

❖ basic recipes
❖ cooking, storing and packaging instructions
❖ completion date, collection point and special transportation instructions
❖ flavour and icing variations, the size or shape of the cake pan required, and tips on cake baking and icing

Give each 'baker' a master plan, with their recipes and variations ticked, together with the quantities she or he has agreed to make.

Most baked goods can be made then frozen without icing. If you ice cakes while still frozen they will set faster.

Arrange to have all your baked goods delivered to a central point for packaging prettily the day before.

For biscuits, collect old tins and boxes to cover in fabric or small cellophane bags attractively tied with curling ribbon.

To wrap cakes, cut a circle of strong cardboard 2 cm larger than the cake. Cover the cardboard with a doily and place the cake on it. Taking care not to touch the icing, gather up the cellophane over the cake and tie with ribbon. Use cake boxes for larger cakes which may be difficult to wrap.

PRICES

Keep prices below local retail prices. The lower the cost of ingredients, the higher your profits will be. If your ingredients aren't donated, buy them in bulk from a wholesaler. Price each item clearly.

DECORATION

Decorating the stall can be lots of fun. Keep the feeling light and airy – like your cakes! If you can, incorporate shelving into the stall (painted bricks and wooden planks are cheap and effective) to give your display height and depth. Borrow baskets to hold biscuits packed in cellophane bags or stack boxed biscuits around the stall.

Keep a variety of cakes and slices on display at all times. Keep a supply of cakes in a cool place to replenish stocks during the day.

❖
BEST EVER CHOCOLATE CAKE

- ☐ ³/₄ **cup (90 g) cocoa**
- ☐ 1¹/₂ **cups (375 mL) boiling water**
- ☐ **185 g butter**
- ☐ 1³/₄ **cup (435 g) caster sugar**
- ☐ **2 tablespoons raspberry jam**
- ☐ **3 eggs**
- ☐ **300 g self-raising flour**

CHOCOLATE MOCHA ICING
- ☐ **120 g butter**
- ☐ **2 cups (335 g) icing sugar, sifted**
- ☐ 1¹/₂ **tablespoons cocoa, sifted**
- ☐ **2 teaspoons instant coffee**
- ☐ **2 tablespoons milk**

1 Combine cocoa and boiling water, mix to dissolve. Allow to cool completely.
2 Cream butter, sugar and jam until light and fluffy. Beat in eggs one at a time, adding a little flour with each egg. Fold in remaining flour and cocoa mixture alternately.
3 Spoon mixture into two greased and lined sandwich pans. Bake at 180°C for 35 minutes or until cooked.
4 To make icing, place butter in a small mixing bowl. Beat until creamy. Add icing sugar a little at a time, beating well after each addition. Combine cocoa and coffee and mix to a smooth paste with milk, then whisk into icing.
5 Ice cake when cold.

Best Ever Chocolate Cake

Spread one layer of cake with icing.

Top with second cake layer. Cover top and sides of cake with icing.

Decorate cake with glace cherries and silver dragees.

❖ BASIC BUTTER CAKE

Add interest to the cake stall by cooking cakes in differently shaped pans. The following recipe works perfectly using the cake pans and cooking times we have given in the chart.

- ☐ **125 g butter**
- ☐ **1 teaspoon vanilla essence**
- ☐ **³/₄ cup (185 g) caster sugar**
- ☐ **2 eggs**
- ☐ **1¹/₂ cups (185 g) plain flour, sifted**
- ☐ **1¹/₂ teaspoons baking powder**
- ☐ **¹/₂ cup (125 mL) milk**

1   Cream butter and vanilla in a small mixing bowl until light and fluffy. Add sugar gradually, beating well after each addition.
2   Beat in eggs one at a time and fold in. Combine flour and baking powder alternately with milk. Spoon mixture into prepared cake pan.
3   Bake according to size of cake pan you have chosen.

Basic Butter Cake, Coffee Cake and Apple Cake

PREPARATION
AND COOKING TIMES

PAN SIZE	PREPARATION	TEMPERATURE	COOKING TIME (minutes)
20 cm ring pan	Grease and line	180°C	40
20 cm deep round pan	Grease and line	180°C	50
20 cm baba pan	Lightly greased	180°C	40
14 cm x 21 cm loaf pan	Grease and line	180°C	60
2 x 8 cm x 26 cm bar pans	Grease and line	180°C	35
24 patty pans	Paper patty cake cases	200°C	15

COOK'S TIP

1   Make sure your butter and eggs are at room temperature before you start.

2   Use caster sugar as it will give your cake a finer texture because it is absorbed by the butter and eggs more rapidly.

3   Use the type of flour the recipe specifies.

4   Cook cakes in the centre of the oven. You can cook more than one cake at a time. Place them on the same shelf, making sure that the pans do not touch each other, the sides or back of the oven, or the oven door when closed. Reverse positions of cake pans halfway through cooking.

5   Grease cake pans with melted butter. Brush evenly over base and sides of pan with a pastry brush then line the base with greaseproof or baking paper.

6   Don't use substitute ingredients as the result will be entirely different.

BUTTER CAKE VARIATIONS

APPLE CAKE

Spread two-thirds of the cake mixture into the prepared cake pan. Top with $^1/_2$ cup (200 g) stewed apple, then remaining cake mixture. Bake according to cake pan size. Stand 10 minutes before turning out.

ORANGE CAKE

Replace vanilla with 2 teaspoons grated orange rind when creaming butter. Substitute 4 tablespoons orange juice for milk. Bake according to cake pan size. Stand 5 minutes before turning out.

COFFEE CAKE

Replace vanilla with 1 tablespoon instant coffee dissolved in 1 tablespoon boiling water. Cool then cream with butter. Bake according to cake pan size. Stand 5 minutes before turning out.

COCONUT CAKE

Replace vanilla with $^1/_2$ teaspoon coconut essence and add $^1/_2$ cup (45 g) desiccated coconut with flour and baking powder. Bake according to pan size. Stand 5 minutes before turning out.

COOK'S TIP

Test your cake just before the end of cooking time. Insert a skewer into the thickest part of the cake. If it comes away clean, your cake is cooked. If there is still cake mixture on the skewer, cook 5 minutes more then test again.

Alternatively, you can gently press the top of cake with your fingertips. When cooked, the depression will spring back quickly. When the cake starts to leave the sides of pan, it is also a good indication that cake is cooked.

BANANA CAKE

Omit milk and add 3 small very ripe mashed bananas to creamed butter and egg mixture. Combine flour, baking powder and 1 teaspoon bicarbonate of soda and fold into butter and egg mixture. Bake according to pan size. Stand 5 minutes before turning out.

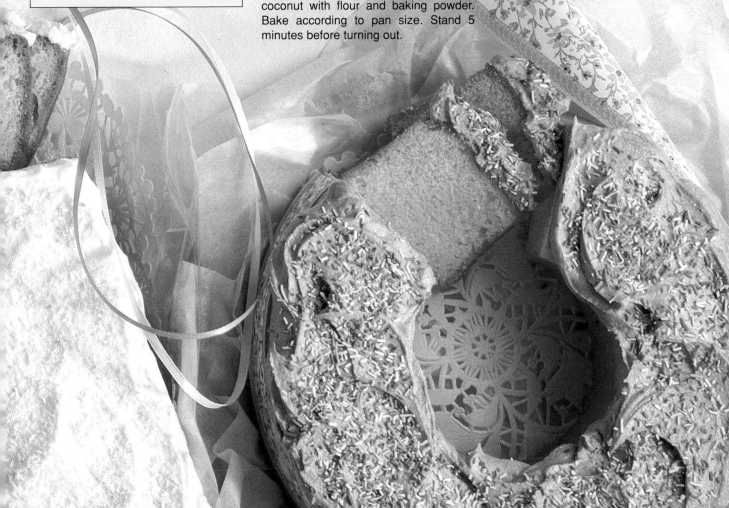

COOK'S TIP

1   Butter icing can be used as a filling for cakes or made to a thicker consistency for piping.

2   Sift all dry ingredients to remove lumps.

3   Beat butter well before adding icing sugar.

4   Make sure butter, eggs and cream cheese are at room temperature.

5   To soften cream cheese, leave at room temperature. To soften in the microwave, remove foil wrap, place in a microwave-safe dish and cook on HIGH (100%) for 20 seconds.

THE ICING ON THE CAKE

❖

LEMON CREAM CHEESE FROSTING

- ☐ **125 g cream cheese**
- ☐ **1 teaspoon grated lemon rind**
- ☐ **1¹/₂ cup (250 g) icing sugar, sifted**
- ☐ **2 teaspooons lemon juice**

Beat cream cheese in a small mixing bowl until creamy. Add lemon rind, icing sugar and lemon juice and mix well.

❖

CHOCOLATE FROSTING

- ☐ **90 g butter**
- ☐ **1¹/₂ cups (250 g) icing sugar, sifted**
- ☐ **1 tablespoon cocoa, sifted**
- ☐ **2 tablespoons cream**

Beat butter in a small bowl until creamy. Add icing sugar, cocoa and cream. Beat until frosting is a spreadable consistency.

Coconut Cake, Banana Cake and Orange Cake (recipes, page 11)

Cake decorating equipment

❖

COFFEE FROSTING

- ☐ **60 g butter**
- ☐ **1¹/₂ cups (250 g) icing sugar, sifted**
- ☐ **2 teaspoons instant coffee, dissolved in 1 tablespoon boiling water**

Beat butter in a small mixing bowl until creamy. Add icing sugar and cooled coffee mixture and beat until frosting is a spreadable consistency.

❖

ORANGE CREAM FROSTING

- ☐ **60 g cream cheese**
- ☐ **2 tablespoons cream**
- ☐ **1 teaspoon grated orange rind**
- ☐ **1¹/₂ cups (250 g) icing sugar, sifted**

Beat cream cheese, cream and orange rind in a small mixing bowl until creamy. Add icing sugar and beat until smooth.

COOK'S TIP

Always use an icing sugar mixture unless recipe states otherwise because pure icing sugar sets too hard. Flavourings that can be used in icing are: melted chocolate, orange juice and orange rind, lemon juice and lemon rind, toppings and sauces, coffee, instant coffee, flavoured essences, coconut.

*Quick Mix Fruit Cake and
Zucchini and Walnut Loaf*

❖

QUICK MIX FRUIT CAKE

- ☐ **125 g butter, melted**
- ☐ **750 g mixed dried fruit**
- ☐ **¹/₂ cup (85 g) brown sugar**
- ☐ **2 tablespoons raspberry jam**
- ☐ **2 eggs, lightly beaten**
- ☐ **¹/₂ cup (125 mL) sweet sherry**
- ☐ **³/₄ cup (90 g) plain flour, sifted**
- ☐ **3 tablespoons self-raising flour, sifted**
- ☐ **125 g blanched almonds**

1   Place butter, fruit, sugar, jam, eggs, sherry and flour in a large bowl and mix until all ingredients are combined.
2   Spoon mixture into a greased 20 cm ring pan. Top with almonds and bake at 160°C for 1¹/₂ hours. Cover with foil and cool in pan.

❖

ZUCCHINI AND WALNUT LOAF

- ☐ **125 g butter**
- ☐ **3 tablespoons brown sugar**
- ☐ **3 tablespoons golden syrup**
- ☐ **1 teaspoon mixed spice**
- ☐ **2 eggs**
- ☐ **3 medium zucchini, grated**
- ☐ **75 g chopped walnuts**
- ☐ **1¹/₂ cups (185 g) wholemeal self-raising flour, sifted**
- ☐ **¹/₂ cup (60 g) white self-raising flour, sifted**
- ☐ **¹/₂ cup (125 mL) buttermilk**

1   Cream butter, sugar and syrup in a small mixing bowl until light and fluffy. Beat in spice and eggs, then stir in zucchini and walnuts. Fold in flours alternately with buttermilk.
2   Spoon mixture into a greased and lined 25 cm x 15 cm loaf pan and bake at 180°C for 40-50 minutes or until cooked. Stand 5 minutes before turning out on a wire rack to cool.

COOK'S TIP

A good fruit cake should be nice and moist. You can achieve this by using ingredients such as brown sugar and syrup. Soaking fruit in alcohol before adding to cake mixture makes your fruit cake taste delicious as well as preventing it from drying out.

A combination of flours can be used such as plain and wholemeal. Butter is usually well creamed with sugar in most fruit cake recipes before adding dry ingredients.

Cake pans should be double lined with paper due to the longer cooking time to prevent burning.

Fruit cakes keep well for a reasonable period of time in a sealed container.

WHAT WENT WRONG ?

Always take time to measure ingredients accurately. Too much sugar causes sugary, sticky crust and coarse crumbs.

Too much flour results in a cake peaked on top, tough and dry in texture.

Too much liquid will result in a soggy, heavy-textured cake that dips in the centre.

Temperature too high will result in a dry cake, peaked and cracked on top.

Pan position and temperature of the oven are important as is choosing the correct size cake pan. Cake pans that are too small will produce a heavy cake with deep cracks over the surface.

❖ LAMINGTONS

Makes 12

- ☐ **125 g butter**
- ☐ **³/₄ cup (185 g) caster sugar**
- ☐ **1 teaspoon vanilla essence**
- ☐ **2 eggs**
- ☐ **1 cup (125 g) self-raising flour, sifted**
- ☐ **1 cup (125 g) plain flour, sifted**
- ☐ **1 teaspoon baking powder**
- ☐ **¹/₂ cup (125 mL) milk**

CHOCOLATE ICING
- ☐ **3¹/₂ cups (590 g) icing sugar, sifted**
- ☐ **3¹/₂ tablespoons cocoa, sifted**
- ☐ **6-8 tablespoons warm water**
- ☐ **coconut**

1 Cream together butter, sugar and vanilla in a small mixing bowl until light and fluffy. Beat in eggs. Combine self-raising flour, plain flour and baking powder and fold in alternately with milk.

Lamingtons

2 Spoon mixture into a greased and lined 28 cm x 18 cm shallow cake pan. Bake at 180°C for 30-35 minutes or until cooked. Stand 5 minutes before turning out on a wire rack to cool.

3 To make chocolate icing, combine icing sugar and cocoa in a large mixing bowl. Pour in water and mix to a smooth consistency.

4 Cut cake into squares and dip into chocolate icing then toss in coconut. Place on greaseproof paper to set.

COOK'S TIP

Place coconut and icing in medium-depth trays so that the coconut does not spill. Have a wire rack handy either positioned over a tray or on greaseproof paper to catch excess icing. Use tongs or two forks for dipping cake into icing. Drain on the rack for a few minutes then roll in coconut.

❖ GINGERBREAD FAMILY

Makes a family of four plus a dog and cat

- [ ] **125 g butter**
- [ ] **¹/₂ cup (85 g) brown sugar**
- [ ] **1 egg**
- [ ] **1 cup (125 g) plain flour, sifted**
- [ ] **1¹/₂ cups (185 g) self-raising flour**
- [ ] **1 tablespoon ground ginger**
- [ ] **2 tablespoons honey**
- [ ] **extra ¹/₄ cup (30 g) plain flour**

ROYAL ICING
- [ ] **1 egg white**
- [ ] **1¹/₂ cups (250 g) pure icing sugar, sifted**
- [ ] **a little lemon juice**
- [ ] **food colouring**

1   Cream butter and sugar in a small mixing bowl until light and fluffy. Beat in egg. Combine flour, bicarbonate of soda and ginger and fold into mixture. Add honey and mix well.

2   Sprinkle extra ¼ cup plain flour onto a surface and knead mixture until soft but not sticky. Chill for 30 minutes. Divide into four portions and roll each portion out to 3 mm thickness.

3   Cut shapes with gingerbread cookie cutters or make cardboard templates. Make two large shapes (Dad and Mum) and two smaller shapes (children). Using a spatula, carefully lift gingerbread figures onto lightly greased oven trays. Re-roll remaining scraps and use to make a dog and cat. Bake at 180°C for 10 minutes. Cool on trays.

4   To make icing, place egg white in a mixing bowl and beat with a wooden spoon. Stir in icing sugar one tablespoon at a time, beating well after each addition. When icing reaches piping consistency, stir in a few drops of lemon juice and desired food colouring.

5   Spoon icing into a small freezer bag and snip off one corner. Use as a piping bag to place features and clothes on biscuits.

Gingerbread Family

Roll out dough to 3 mm thickness.

Cut shapes with gingerbread cookie cutters.

COOK'S TIP

When making biscuits, butter should always be at room temperature. Never overstir biscuit mixture. Flat trays are best for cooking, preferably lined with baking paper.

Most biscuits crisp on cooling so you don't need to overcook them to make them crisp. Biscuits should be left on the tray to cool and removed when firm.

Position biscuits in the top half of the oven for cooking. Open the door and check during cooking. Don't be afraid to turn the tray as some ovens tend to be hotter towards the back.

When positioning biscuits on the tray, allow room for the mixture to expand.

Biscuits should be even in colour, usually a light straw colour. If you position the biscuits towards the bottom of the oven, they will burn on the base.

Pipe on facial features and clothes.

❖
HONEY MALT BARS

Makes 20 bars

- ☐ **2 cups (250 g) self-raising flour, sifted**
- ☐ **1 cup (90 g) rolled oats**
- ☐ **1 cup (95 g) coconut**
- ☐ **3 cups (250 g) crushed Weet-Bix**
- ☐ **1 cup (170 g) brown sugar**
- ☐ **250 g butter, melted**
- ☐ **4 tablespoons honey**

MOCHA ICING
- ☐ **1 cup (75 g) icing sugar, sifted**
- ☐ **2 teaspoons cocoa**
- ☐ **2 teaspoons instant coffee**
- ☐ **15 g butter**
- ☐ **about 1 tablespoon water**

1   Place flour, oats, coconut, Weet-Bix and sugar in a large mixing bowl. Mix well to combine. Blend together butter and honey and stir into dry ingredients.
2   Press mixture into a greased 26 cm x 18 cm shallow cake pan. Bake at 180°C for 35-40 minutes or until golden brown. Cool in pan at room temperature.
3   To make mocha icing, combine icing sugar, cocoa, coffee and butter in a heatproof bowl. Add water and mix to a stiff consistency. Place bowl over a saucepan of hot water and stir until icing is of spreading consistency. Spread icing over slice and cut into fingers when set.

❖
MUESLI BARS

Makes 20 bars

- ☐ **1¹/₂ cups (180 g) natural muesli**
- ☐ **¹/₂ cup (50 g) desiccated coconut**
- ☐ **¹/₂ cup (60 g) wholemeal plain flour, sifted**
- ☐ **¹/₂ cup (60 g) pine nuts**
- ☐ **³/₄ cup (125 g) sultanas**
- ☐ **3 tablespoons sesame seeds**
- ☐ **¹/₂ cup (85 g) brown sugar**
- ☐ **125 g butter, melted**
- ☐ **2 tablespoons golden syrup**
- ☐ **2 eggs, lightly beaten**

1   Combine muesli, coconut, flour, nuts, sultanas, sesame seeds and sugar in a large mixing bowl. Blend together butter, golden syrup and eggs and stir into dry ingredients.

Honey Malt Bars, Muesli Bars, Almond Cookies, Hazelnut Fingers, Chocolate Chip Cookies and Orange Shortbread

2   Press mixture into a greased 28 cm x 18 cm shallow cake pan. Bake at 180°C 20-25 minutes. Cool at room temperature. Cut into finger lengths when cold.

❖
ALMOND COOKIES

Makes 36

- ☐ **125 g butter**
- ☐ **1 cup (250 g) caster sugar**
- ☐ **¹/₂ teaspoon almond essence**
- ☐ **1 egg**
- ☐ **1 cup (125 g) plain flour, sifted**
- ☐ **1 cup (125 g) self-raising flour, sifted**
- ☐ **¹/₂ cup (50 g) desiccated coconut**
- ☐ **¹/₂ cup (90 g) chopped glace cherries**
- ☐ **1 cup (125 g) chopped almonds**

1   Beat butter and sugar in a small mixing bowl until creamy. Beat in almond essence and egg then fold in flour, coconut and cherries. Cover and refrigerate for 2 hours.
2   Roll heaped teaspoonfuls of mixture into balls. Dip one half of each ball into chopped almonds and arrange almond side up on a greased oven tray, spacing biscuits apart. Flatten each biscuit very slightly and bake at 180°C for 12-15 minutes or until golden. Remove from tray and cool on a wire rack.

❖
HAZELNUT FINGERS

Makes 45

- ☐ **3 egg whites**
- ☐ **³/₄ cup (185 g) caster sugar**
- ☐ **250 g ground hazelnuts**
- ☐ **¹/₂ teaspoon almond essence**
- ☐ **3 tablespoons cornflour, sifted**
- ☐ **3 tablespoons plain flour, sifted**
- ☐ **100 g plain, dark chocolate**
- ☐ **30 g copha (vegetable shortening)**

1   Beat egg whites in a small mixing bowl until soft peaks form. Add sugar a little at a time, beating well after each addition until mixture is thick and glossy.
2   Fold in hazelnuts, essence, cornflour and flour. Place mixture in a piping bag fitted with a plain tube and pipe 5 cm lengths on greased oven trays. Bake at 180°C for 10 minutes. Cool on a wire rack.
3   Combine chocolate and copha. Melt over hot water. Dip biscuit ends in chocolate mixture. Place on aluminium foil to set.

❖
CHOCOLATE CHIP COOKIES

Makes 36

- ☐ **125 g butter**
- ☐ **¹/₂ cup (125 g) caster sugar**
- ☐ **¹/₂ cup (85 g) brown sugar**
- ☐ **¹/₂ teaspoon coconut essence**
- ☐ **1 egg**
- ☐ **³/₄ cup (90 g) plain flour, sifted**
- ☐ **¹/₂ cup (50 g) coconut**
- ☐ **125 g chocolate chips**
- ☐ **100 g plain, dark chocolate, melted**

1   Beat butter, sugars and essence in a small mixing bowl until creamy. Beat in egg, then fold in flour, coconut and chocolate chips.
2   Place teaspoonfuls of mixture on greased oven trays, allowing room for spreading. Bake at 180°C for 15 minutes. Remove from trays and cool on a wire rack. Pipe melted chocolate in three thin lines over top of biscuits.

❖
ORANGE SHORTBREAD

Makes 20 squares

- ☐ **250 g butter**
- ☐ **¹/₂ cup (125 g) plus 1 tablespoon caster sugar**
- ☐ **3 teaspoons orange juice**
- ☐ **1 teaspoon orange rind**
- ☐ **2 cups (250 g) plain flour, sifted**
- ☐ **¹/₂ cup (90 g) rice flour, sifted**

1   Beat butter and ¹/₂ cup sugar in a small mixing bowl until creamy. Beat in orange juice and rind, combine flours and fold in.
2   Spread mixture into a greased 20 cm square cake pan. Mark into squares, prick with a fork, sprinkle over remaining caster sugar Bake at 180°C for 40-45 minutes or until light golden brown. When cold cut into squares.

MICROWAVE **I**T

When making Hazelnut Fingers, place chocolate and copha (vegetable shortening) in a microwave-safe bowl. Cook on HIGH (100%) for 1-2 minutes or until chocolate is melted. Stir after every 30 seconds. Be careful not to overcook, as chocolate will burn easily.

weet stall temptations

A child's delight – this stall is a treasure trove of toffee apples, honeycomb, fudge, Turkish delight and lots more!

Sweet making can be an exacting task – so enlist the help of experienced sweet makers or good cooks. It is important for consistency of quality that everyone uses reliable, well-tested recipes. When you have decided on the variety of sweets you and your team are going to make, compile master plans including all the recipes, together with cooking, storing and delivery instructions. Give each sweetmaker a copy, highlighting the recipes they have agreed to make.

Package your sweets at a central point a day or two before the fete. Beg or buy a selection of clear plastic boxes, cellophane bags and other suitable wrappings. Pretty tins and covered chocolate boxes are also excellent ideas, but start collecting them early to ensure you have enough. Decorate your packages with colourful curling ribbons and silk flowers.

PRICES

It is vital to keep costs to a minimum so that you can keep your prices below retail. Make sure there is a good selection of cheap treats for children. Adults also love to indulge in their favourite confectionery and will usually pay that little bit extra for beautiful wrapping and presentation.

DECORATION

Decorating the sweet stall is a treat in itself. Make the most of the stall by winding ribbon around the support poles and taping bags of sweets onto them. Hang toffee apples on strings from the top of the stall and use baskets and shelving to add interest to the display.

COOK'S TIP

Use a deep, heavy-based saucepan made of aluminium, copper or stainless steel.

Dissolve the sugar in the water or liquid very slowly over low heat. Do not allow it to boil until sugar is completely dissolved. After boiling begins, remove any crystals that form on the sides of pan with a clean brush dipped in warm water. Do not stir after boiling point is reached unless recipe states otherwise.

Most toffees and candies are better when made in dry, cool weather as high humidity can affect cooking times and temperatures. Temperature should be 1-2 degrees higher on very humid days.

Try not to scrape dregs of toffee from the pan as the crystallisation rate between this and the free flowing portion will differ because of the greater amount of heat applied to the base of the pan.

❖
TOFFEE APPLES

The thick wooden skewers used for the toffee apples can be purchased from Asian food shops and decorating suppliers. Dip carefully as air bubbles form if you dip too quickly.

Makes 10

- [ ] **4 cups (1 kg) sugar**
- [ ] **250 g butter**
- [ ] **4 tablespoons white vinegar**
- [ ] **4 tablespoons boiling water**
- [ ] **$\frac{1}{2}$ teaspoon red food colouring**
- [ ] **10 small green apples, washed and dried**
- [ ] **10 thick wooden skewers**

1   Combine sugar, butter, vinegar, boiling water and food colouring in a heavy-based saucepan. Cook over a low heat, stirring until sugar dissolves.
2   Increase heat and boil without stirring for about 10 minutes or until mixture reaches the hard crack stage or 150°C on a sugar thermometer. Remove from heat and allow bubbles to subside.
3   Pierce apples through the centre with the wooden skewers. With the pan tilted to one side carefully dip an apple into the toffee and twist slowly to completely coat. Remove apple slowly and twirl over pan to remove excess toffee. Dip coated apple into iced water to harden toffee then place on an oiled oven tray to set. Repeat with remaining apples. If toffee becomes too thick to work with, place over a moderate heat.

COOK'S TIP
Toffee apples must be made as close to the day as possible and stored in airtight containers to stop them sweating. Fudge needs to be kept away from sunlight. Chocolate items should be stored in the refrigerator until required.

Toffee Apples

Pierce apples through the centre with wooden skewers.

With the pan tilted to one side carefully dip apple.

Dip coated apple into iced water.

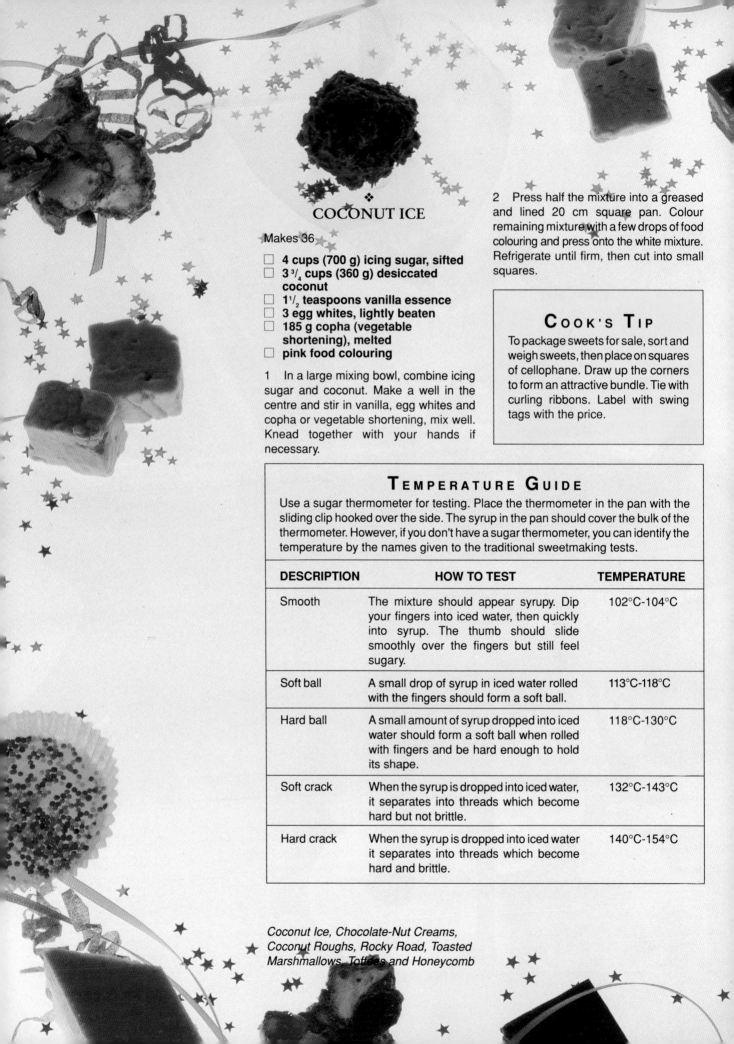

❖
COCONUT ICE

Makes 36

- ☐ **4 cups (700 g) icing sugar, sifted**
- ☐ **3 ³/₄ cups (360 g) desiccated coconut**
- ☐ **1¹/₂ teaspoons vanilla essence**
- ☐ **3 egg whites, lightly beaten**
- ☐ **185 g copha (vegetable shortening), melted**
- ☐ **pink food colouring**

1   In a large mixing bowl, combine icing sugar and coconut. Make a well in the centre and stir in vanilla, egg whites and copha or vegetable shortening, mix well. Knead together with your hands if necessary.

2   Press half the mixture into a greased and lined 20 cm square pan. Colour remaining mixture with a few drops of food colouring and press onto the white mixture. Refrigerate until firm, then cut into small squares.

COOK'S TIP

To package sweets for sale, sort and weigh sweets, then place on squares of cellophane. Draw up the corners to form an attractive bundle. Tie with curling ribbons. Label with swing tags with the price.

TEMPERATURE GUIDE

Use a sugar thermometer for testing. Place the thermometer in the pan with the sliding clip hooked over the side. The syrup in the pan should cover the bulk of the thermometer. However, if you don't have a sugar thermometer, you can identify the temperature by the names given to the traditional sweetmaking tests.

DESCRIPTION	HOW TO TEST	TEMPERATURE
Smooth	The mixture should appear syrupy. Dip your fingers into iced water, then quickly into syrup. The thumb should slide smoothly over the fingers but still feel sugary.	102°C-104°C
Soft ball	A small drop of syrup in iced water rolled with the fingers should form a soft ball.	113°C-118°C
Hard ball	A small amount of syrup dropped into iced water should form a soft ball when rolled with fingers and be hard enough to hold its shape.	118°C-130°C
Soft crack	When the syrup is dropped into iced water, it separates into threads which become hard but not brittle.	132°C-143°C
Hard crack	When the syrup is dropped into iced water it separates into threads which become hard and brittle.	140°C-154°C

Coconut Ice, Chocolate-Nut Creams, Coconut Roughs, Rocky Road, Toasted Marshmallows, Toffees and Honeycomb

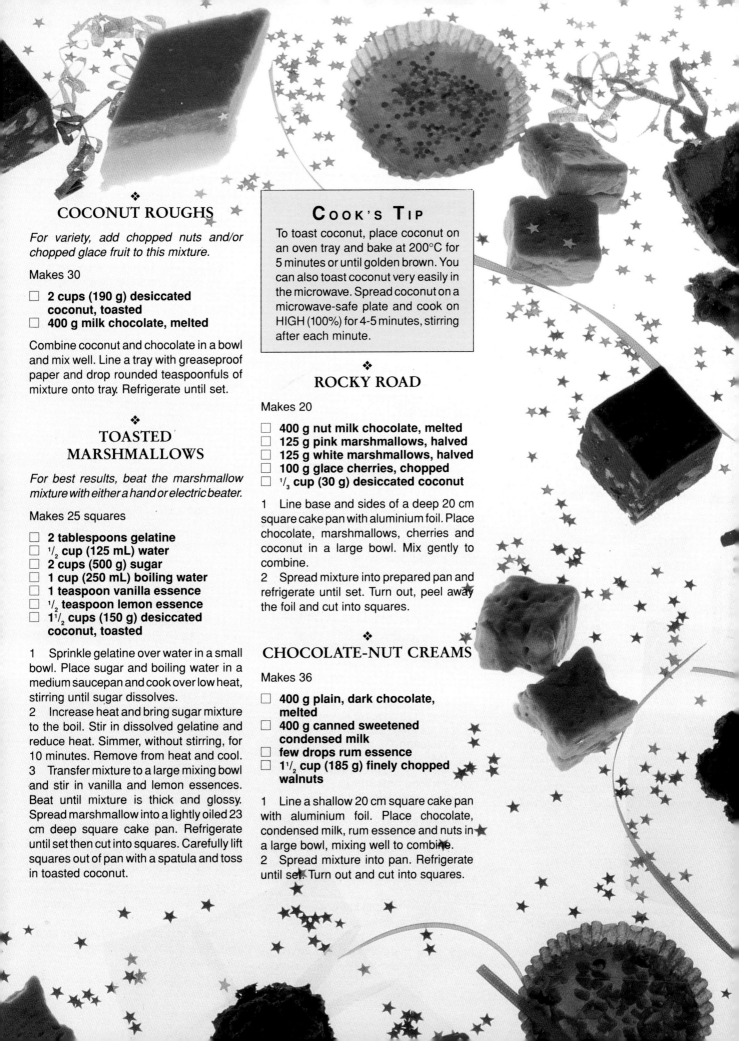

COCONUT ROUGHS

For variety, add chopped nuts and/or chopped glace fruit to this mixture.

Makes 30

- ☐ **2 cups (190 g) desiccated coconut, toasted**
- ☐ **400 g milk chocolate, melted**

Combine coconut and chocolate in a bowl and mix well. Line a tray with greaseproof paper and drop rounded teaspoonfuls of mixture onto tray. Refrigerate until set.

TOASTED MARSHMALLOWS

For best results, beat the marshmallow mixture with either a hand or electric beater.

Makes 25 squares

- ☐ **2 tablespoons gelatine**
- ☐ **$^1/_2$ cup (125 mL) water**
- ☐ **2 cups (500 g) sugar**
- ☐ **1 cup (250 mL) boiling water**
- ☐ **1 teaspoon vanilla essence**
- ☐ **$^1/_2$ teaspoon lemon essence**
- ☐ **$1^1/_2$ cups (150 g) desiccated coconut, toasted**

1 Sprinkle gelatine over water in a small bowl. Place sugar and boiling water in a medium saucepan and cook over low heat, stirring until sugar dissolves.

2 Increase heat and bring sugar mixture to the boil. Stir in dissolved gelatine and reduce heat. Simmer, without stirring, for 10 minutes. Remove from heat and cool.

3 Transfer mixture to a large mixing bowl and stir in vanilla and lemon essences. Beat until mixture is thick and glossy. Spread marshmallow into a lightly oiled 23 cm deep square cake pan. Refrigerate until set then cut into squares. Carefully lift squares out of pan with a spatula and toss in toasted coconut.

COOK'S TIP

To toast coconut, place coconut on an oven tray and bake at 200°C for 5 minutes or until golden brown. You can also toast coconut very easily in the microwave. Spread coconut on a microwave-safe plate and cook on HIGH (100%) for 4-5 minutes, stirring after each minute.

ROCKY ROAD

Makes 20

- ☐ **400 g nut milk chocolate, melted**
- ☐ **125 g pink marshmallows, halved**
- ☐ **125 g white marshmallows, halved**
- ☐ **100 g glace cherries, chopped**
- ☐ **$^1/_3$ cup (30 g) desiccated coconut**

1 Line base and sides of a deep 20 cm square cake pan with aluminium foil. Place chocolate, marshmallows, cherries and coconut in a large bowl. Mix gently to combine.

2 Spread mixture into prepared pan and refrigerate until set. Turn out, peel away the foil and cut into squares.

CHOCOLATE-NUT CREAMS

Makes 36

- ☐ **400 g plain, dark chocolate, melted**
- ☐ **400 g canned sweetened condensed milk**
- ☐ **few drops rum essence**
- ☐ **$1^1/_2$ cup (185 g) finely chopped walnuts**

1 Line a shallow 20 cm square cake pan with aluminium foil. Place chocolate, condensed milk, rum essence and nuts in a large bowl, mixing well to combine.

2 Spread mixture into pan. Refrigerate until set. Turn out and cut into squares.

Turkish Delight

❖
TOFFEES

You can make toffees up to a week in advance and store them in airtight containers, but do not freeze.

Makes 12

- ☐ **2 cups (500 g) sugar**
- ☐ **1 cup (250 mL) water**
- ☐ **15 g butter**
- ☐ **2 teaspoons vinegar**
- ☐ **2 teaspoons honey**
- ☐ **chopped nuts or hundreds and thousands**

1   Place sugar, water, butter, vinegar and honey in a medium saucepan and cook over a low heat, stirring until sugar dissolves.

2   Increase heat and boil without stirring for about 12 minutes until mixture is golden brown and reaches the hard crack stage or 154°C on a sugar thermometer. Remove from heat and allow bubbles to subside.

3   Pour toffee into paper patty cases and sprinkle with chopped nuts or hundreds and thousands.

❖
HONEYCOMB

Makes 30 squares

- ☐ **1 cup (250 g) sugar**
- ☐ **1 tablespoon golden syrup**
- ☐ **1 tablespoon vinegar**
- ☐ **15 g butter**
- ☐ **¹/₂ teaspoon bicarbonate of soda**

---

1   Combine sugar, golden syrup, vinegar and butter in a heavy-based saucepan and cook over medium heat, stirring until sugar dissolves.

2   Increase heat and boil without stirring until mixture reaches hard crack stage or 149°C on a sugar thermometer and a few drops of mixture snap and crackle and immediately harden when dropped into iced water.

3   Remove pan from heat and add bicarbonate of soda, stirring until mixture swells. Pour into a lightly oiled 23 cm square cake pan. When almost set, cut into squares.

❖
TURKISH DELIGHT

Makes about 18 squares

- ☐ **2 cups (500 g) sugar**
- ☐ **1¹/₂ cups (375 mL) cold water**
- ☐ **¹/₄ teaspoon cream of tartar**
- ☐ **4 tablespoons cornflour**
- ☐ **1 cup (175 g) icing sugar, sifted**
- ☐ **2 cups (500 mL) boiling water**
- ☐ **2 tablespoons honey**
- ☐ **1 teaspoon lemon juice**
- ☐ **2 tablespoons rosewater essence**
- ☐ **pink food colouring**
- ☐ **icing sugar for coating**

1   Place sugar and ¹/₂ cup (125 mL) cold water in a heavy-based saucepan and cook over low heat, stirring until sugar dissolves. Brush any sugar from the side of the pan with a pastry brush dipped in cold water.

2   Increase heat and boil sugar mixture, without stirring, for about 8 minutes, until mixture reaches soft ball stage or 118°C on a sugar thermometer. Add cream of tartar, remove from the heat and set aside.

---

3   Blend cornflour and icing sugar with remaining cold water in a heavy-based saucepan and stir until smooth. Pour over boiling water, then stir in sugar syrup until the mixture forms a lump. Stir until lump dissolves. Return to medium heat, stirring until mixture boils and thickens.

4   Reduce heat to low and cook mixture a further 1¹/₄ hours, stirring occasionally until mixture is pale golden. Add honey, lemon juice, rosewater and a few drops of food colouring and blend thoroughly.

5   Pour mixture into a lightly oiled 18 cm square cake pan and stand, uncovered, at room temperature for 24 hours or until set. Cut Turkish Delight into squares with an oiled knife. Toss each square in sifted icing sugar. Store between sheets of waxed paper in an airtight container.

❖
CHOCOLATE-RUM TRUFFLES

If you don't want to use rum in this recipe, substitute rum essence to taste.

Makes about 25

- ☐ **200 g plain, dark chocolate**
- ☐ **30 g butter**
- ☐ **2 egg yolks**
- ☐ **2 tablespoons rum**
- ☐ **1 tablespoon cream**
- ☐ **cocoa powder**

1   Melt chocolate and butter in a bowl over hot water. Remove from heat. Add egg yolks, rum and cream, stirring until mixture is thick enough to handle.

2   Chill mixture slightly until firm enough to form into small balls. Roll in sifted cocoa powder. Cover and refrigerate until firm.

❖
ALMOND TRUFFLES

Makes about 20

- ☐ **30 g plain, dark chocolate**
- ☐ **125 g marzipan**
- ☐ **2 tablespoons ground almonds**
- ☐ **2 teaspoons vanilla essence**
- ☐ **1 teaspoon sweet sherry**
- ☐ **finely chopped almonds**

1   Melt chocolate in a bowl over hot water and combine with marzipan, ground almonds, vanilla and sherry.

2   Knead mixture well and form into small balls. Toss in chopped almonds, cover and refrigerate until firm.

❖ APRICOT BALLS

These apricot balls can be made up to one week in advance. Store them in an airtight container between layers of waxed paper.

Makes 30

- ☐ ¹/₂ **cup (70 g) dried apricots**
- ☐ ¹/₂ **cup (100 g) pitted prunes**
- ☐ ¹/₄ **cup (40 g) raisins**
- ☐ 3¹/₂ **tablespoons Grand Marnier (or orange juice)**
- ☐ **2 teaspoons grated orange rind**
- ☐ 1¹/₃ **cups (120 g) desiccated coconut**
- ☐ ³/₄ **cup (90 g) chopped almonds**
- ☐ ³/₄ **cup (185 g) sugar**

1   Place apricots, prunes and raisins in a bowl, pour over 3 tablespoons Grand Marnier and stand for 1 hour. Transfer to the bowl of a food processor and process until finely chopped.

2   Combine chopped fruit with orange rind, 75 g coconut and nuts. Form mixture into bite-size balls. Add a little extra Grand Marnier if necessary to make the mixture easier to mould. Mix together remaining coconut and sugar, and roll apricot balls in this mixture to coat.

Apricot Balls, Truffles, Rum Balls, Creamy Caramels and Almond-Pecan Brittle

❖ ALMOND-PECAN BRITTLE

Makes 25

- ☐ **225 g blanched almonds**
- ☐ **125 g pecan nuts**
- ☐ 1¹/₂ **cups (375 g) sugar**
- ☐ ³/₄ **cup (125 g) brown sugar**
- ☐ ¹/₂ **cup (180 g) golden syrup**
- ☐ ¹/₂ **cup (125 mL) water**
- ☐ **60 g butter**
- ☐ ¹/₄ **teaspoon bicarbonate of soda**

1   Place almonds and pecans on an oven tray and bake at 180°C for 5 minutes or until light golden brown. Remove from oven and set aside.

2   Combine sugars, syrup and water in a heavy-based saucepan and cook over medium heat, stirring until sugar dissolves. Add butter. Bring to the boil. Boil, without stirring, until mixture reaches hard crack stage or 149⁰C on a sugar thermometer.

3   Stir in bicarbonate of soda and toasted nuts. Pour into a lightly oiled 23 cm cake pan. When almost set, cut into squares.

❖ RUM BALLS

Makes about 60

- ☐ **4 cups (350 g) plain cake crumbs**
- ☐ ³/₄ **cup (125 g) finely chopped raisins**
- ☐ **400 g canned sweetened condensed milk**
- ☐ **2 cups (190 g) desiccated coconut**
- ☐ **2 teaspoons lemon rind**
- ☐ **1 tablespoon lemon juice**
- ☐ **1 tablespoon cocoa powder**
- ☐ **2 tablespoons rum or rum essence**
- ☐ **chocolate sprinkles**

1   Combine cake crumbs, raisins, condensed milk, coconut, lemon rind, juice, cocoa powder and rum in a large bowl and mix well.

2   Form mixture into small balls and toss to coat in chocolate sprinkles. Cover and refrigerate until firm.

❖ CREAMY CARAMELS

Makes 25

- ☐ **1 cup (170 g) brown sugar**
- ☐ **2 tablespoons water**
- ☐ **125 g butter**
- ☐ ¹/₄ **teaspoon vanilla essence**
- ☐ **3 tablespoons cream**

1   Place sugar and water in a heavy-based saucepan and cook over medium heat, stirring until sugar dissolves.

2   Add butter, vanilla and cream, increase heat and boil, without stirring, until mixture reaches hard ball stage or 130⁰C. A few drops will form a soft ball when dropped into iced water.

3   Pour caramel into a lightly oiled 20 cm square cake pan. When almost set, cut into squares.

ourmet stall delicacies

The gourmet food stall offers buyers all the fine produce of a country garden and gourmet restaurant combined — fruity marmalades and jams, delicate herbed oils and vinegars, spicy pickles and relishes, pork pies and pates.

Preparations for your gourmet stall should begin as early as possible with the collection of an interesting selection of bottles, jars and pate pots. Ask for medium-sized jars for jams and chutneys and small jars and pots for mustard. Old vinegar, wine and mint sauce bottles are great for herbed oils and vinegars. Coloured glass detracts from the appeal of the contents.

Ask your team of volunteer gourmet chefs for their specialities to add to your list of goods to make. Once you have decided what to include on your stall, divide your products into categories, such as relishes and chutneys, pastes and pates, and prepare a master plan for each group including:

❖ recipes and ingredients
❖ instructions for bottling and packaging
❖ method of storage until delivery
❖ special tips such as those for jam making

Give each gourmet cook a copy of the master plan with the recipes and quantities they have agreed to make clearly marked.

Collect the goods at least a day or two before the big day to add any final touches and complete the packaging. Cover tops of jars with pretty floral or gingham fabrics. Even small paper doilies can look wonderful. Tie them into place with ribbon or cord. Make decorative labels for all your products, labelling vinegars and oils with tags with a bay leaf or a sprig of herbs attached. Prepare bouquet garni in squares of calico or muslin, gathered and tied with string. Delicious pork pies can be attractively boxed in batches of six, or wrapped individually in cellophane.

PRICES

Aim to offer a range of products at various prices, keeping them under local retail prices wherever possible. If you have kept your costs down, you will be able to sell at very reasonable prices and still make excellent profits.

DECORATION

Decorate the stall in 'gourmet' colours like terracotta, dark green and calico. Use baskets filled with fresh fruit or vegetables or herbs growing in clay pots to add to the pleasant country atmosphere.

When displaying your goods, make the most of their mouth-watering appearance. Arrange brandied apricots beside mint jelly and lemon curd beside strawberry jam. Place small jars at the front of the stand and graduate to larger bottles at the rear. Use baskets or terracotta bowls to present bouquet garnis and other herbs. Keep pates or pork pies well chilled, only displaying a few at a time and replenishing stocks frequently.

❖

PICKLED ONIONS

Pickled onions will be ready to eat after three to four days but have more flavour if left three to four weeks. If making only a few days before selling them, attach a label to the jars giving a 'do not eat before' date, for example, 'Allow flavour to develop fully – these pickled onions will taste best if eaten after (give date)'.

Makes 4 medium (375 mL) jars

☐ **2 kg small pickling onions**
☐ **$^1/_2$ cup (125 g) coarse cooking salt**
☐ **$1^1/_4$ litres white vinegar**
☐ **1 tablespoon sugar**

PICKLING SPICE
☐ **$1^1/_2$ teaspoons whole cloves**
☐ **2 teaspoons whole allspice**
☐ **2 teaspoons whole black peppercorns**
☐ **2 bay leaves**

1   Cover unpeeled onions with boiling water and stand for 2 minutes. Drain and plunge into cold water. Peel onions and combine with salt in a large ceramic bowl. Pour over enough cold water to just cover onions, cover and refrigerate.
2   Place vinegar and sugar in a medium saucepan and bring to the boil.
3   To make pickling spice, place cloves, allspice, peppercorns and bay leaves in several layers of muslin. Tie together to form a bag and drop into boiling vinegar mixture. Cook for 5 minutes, then remove pan from heat and cool mixture 2-3 hours at room temperature. Remove and discard spice bag.
4   Drain onions and rinse under cold running water. Pack firmly into sterilised jars leaving $^1/_2$ cm head space at the top. Pour vinegar over onions and seal jars.

COOK'S TIP

Use clean unchipped jars. Remove any labels. Cold glass will crack if heat is suddenly applied. Before you fill with hot preserve, warm in a low oven until required. Sterilising solution can also be used for jars. Follow packet directions.

COOK'S TIP

Brandied apricots are best stored in a cool, dark place. For full flavour to develop, store for one month before using.

❖

BRANDIED APRICOTS

Makes 3 small (250 mL) jars

- ☐ **2 cups (500 g) sugar**
- ☐ **1 cup (250 mL) water**
- ☐ **1 kg apricots, peeled, halved and stoned**
- ☐ **¼ teaspoon ground nutmeg**
- ☐ **1 cup (250 mL) brandy**

1 Combine sugar and water in a large saucepan. Cook over medium heat, stirring until sugar dissolves. Add apricots and nutmeg, simmering until apricots are just tender.

2 Remove apricots with a slotted spoon and pack tightly in hot sterilised jars. Bring syrup to the boil and continue boiling for about 8 minutes or until reduced by half and light golden brown.

3 Half fill sterilised jars with brandy, then pour over syrup to within 2 cm of the top. Seal when cold.

❖

MINT JELLY

Makes 2 small (250 mL) jars

- ☐ **5 cooking apples, washed and quartered**
- ☐ **1 cup (60 g) loosely packed fresh mint leaves**
- ☐ **3 lemons, sliced**
- ☐ **water**
- ☐ **½ cup (125 mL) cider vinegar**
- ☐ **sugar**
- ☐ **2 tablespoons chopped fresh mint**
- ☐ **green food colouring**

1 Combine apples, mint leaves and lemons in a large saucepan. Pour over enough cold water to just cover apples.

Beautifully packaged gourmet delicacies

Bring to the boil, reduce heat and simmer for 15-20 minutes or until apples are very soft. Add vinegar and simmer a further 5 minutes.

2 Strain mixture through muslin, being careful not to allow any solid matter into the strained liquid. Measure strained liquid and return to cleaned saucepan adding ¾ cup sugar for each cup liquid. Cook over low heat, stirring until sugar dissolves. Increase heat and boil without stirring for 25-30 minutes or until the mixture gels when tested.

3 Stir in chopped mint and colour with a few drops of green food colouring. Pour in hot sterilised jars and seal when cold.

❖ BREAD AND BUTTER CUCUMBERS

Makes 4 medium (375 mL) jars

- ☐ 4 large cucumbers, sliced
- ☐ 2 onions, sliced
- ☐ 1 green capsicum, sliced
- ☐ 4 tablespoons salt
- ☐ water
- ☐ 2¹/₂ cups (625 mL) white vinegar
- ☐ 1¹/₂ cups (375 g) sugar
- ☐ 2 teaspoons mustard seeds
- ☐ 1 teaspoon celery seeds
- ☐ 1 teaspoon mixed spice

1   Combine cucumbers, onions and capsicum in a large glass dish. Sprinkle with salt and pour over enough water to cover vegetables. Stand for 5 hours, then drain and rinse under cold running water.

2   Place vinegar, sugar, mustard seeds, celery seeds and mixed spice in a large saucepan and cook over low heat, stirring until sugar dissolves. Add vegetables and cook over medium heat until mixture boils. Remove from heat.

3   Using tongs and working quickly, pack vegetables tightly into hot sterilised jars. Fill with vinegar mixture to within 1 cm of the top of the jar and seal when cold.

❖ TOMATO RELISH

Store relishes in a cool, dark place. The flavour improves if left for three to four weeks before using.

Makes 3 medium (375 mL) jars

- ☐ 1¹/₂ kg tomatoes, peeled and chopped
- ☐ ¹/₂ cup (125 g) coarse cooking salt

- ☐ 4 onions, chopped
- ☐ 2¹/₂ cups (625 mL) white vinegar
- ☐ 1³/₄ cups (435 g) sugar
- ☐ 4-5 small red chillies, finely chopped
- ☐ 1 tablespoon curry powder
- ☐ 1 tablespoon ground turmeric
- ☐ 2 teaspoons prepared hot mustard
- ☐ 1 teaspoon ground cumin
- ☐ 1 teaspoon garam masala
- ☐ 2 tablespoons plain flour

1   Place tomatoes in a large glass bowl, sprinkle with salt and stand covered overnight.

2   Drain tomatoes and rinse under cold running water, then combine with onions and vinegar in a large saucepan. Bring to the boil, reduce heat and simmer for 10 minutes. Add sugar and chillies, stir until sugar is dissolved then simmer a further 5 minutes.

3   Combine curry powder, turmeric, mustard, cumin, garam masala and flour in a small bowl with enough cold water to make a paste. Whisk into the simmering tomato mixture and cook for 1 hour over low heat, or until mixture thickens, stirring from time to time.

4   Pour mixture into hot sterilised jars and seal when cold.

❖ SPICY APPLE CHUTNEY

Makes 2 large (500 mL) jars

- ☐ 2 tablespoons polyunsaturated oil
- ☐ 1 clove garlic, crushed
- ☐ 1 teaspoon grated fresh ginger
- ☐ 2 fresh chillies, seeded and chopped
- ☐ 2 tablespoons mustard seeds
- ☐ 1 teaspoon five spice powder

- ☐ 1 teaspoon mixed spice
- ☐ 1 teaspoon ground turmeric
- ☐ 15 whole black peppercorns
- ☐ 2 teaspoons ground cumin
- ☐ 8 large cooking apples, peeled, cored and sliced
- ☐ ²/₃ cup (165 mL) white vinegar
- ☐ ¹/₂ cup (125 g) sugar

1   Heat oil in a large saucepan, add garlic, ginger and chillies and cook for 2-3 minutes. Combine mustard seeds, five spice powder, mixed spice, turmeric, peppercorns and cumin. Add to garlic mixture. Cook for 3-4 minutes.

2   Add apples, vinegar and sugar. Simmer, uncovered, until thick, for about 1 hour. Pour chutney into hot sterilised jars and seal when cold.

❖ PLUM JAM

The plums used in this jam recipe are the dark red plums known either as damson or blood plums.

Makes 3 medium (375 mL) jars

- ☐ 1 kg blood plums
- ☐ 1 cup (250 mL) water
- ☐ 1 kg sugar
- ☐ 15 g butter

1   Wash and halve plums, then remove stones. Place plums and water in a large saucepan. Bring to the boil, reduce heat, cover and simmer for 15-20 minutes or until fruit is soft and pulpy.

2   Add sugar, stirring constantly until sugar dissolves. Increase heat and boil, uncovered, for about 20-30 minutes or until jam gels when tested. Stir in butter.

3   Stand for 10 minutes, then pour jam into hot sterilised jars. Seal when cold.

❖ THREE FRUIT MARMALADE

Makes 7 small (250 mL) jars

- ☐ **2 large oranges**
- ☐ **2 limes**
- ☐ **1 large grapefruit**
- ☐ **1 litre water**
- ☐ **7 cups (1³/₄ kg) sugar**

1   Cut unpeeled fruit in half, then slice thinly discarding seeds. Place fruit in a large bowl and pour over water. Cover and stand overnight.

2   Transfer fruit and water to a large saucepan and bring to the boil, then reduce heat and simmer, uncovered, for about 1 hour, until fruit is soft.

3   Add sugar, stirring constantly without boiling, until sugar dissolves. Increase heat and boil, uncovered, without stirring, for about 45 minutes or until marmalade gels when tested on a cold saucer. Stand 10 minutes before pouring into hot sterilised jars seal when cold.

❖ FIG JAM

If you are using ordinary dried figs, pour warm water over them and leave overnight. Drain before using.

Makes 7 small (250 mL) jars

- ☐ **1¹/₂ kg tenderised dried figs**
- ☐ **1 cup (250 mL) water**
- ☐ **3 teaspoons sugar**

1   Remove the stems from the figs and cut into small pieces. Place figs and water in a large saucepan and bring to the boil. Reduce heat and simmer, covered, for about 15-20 minutes or until fruit is soft.

2   Add sugar and stir constantly until sugar dissolves. Increase heat and boil, uncovered, for about 40-50 minutes or until jam gels when tested. Stir in butter.

3   Stand for 10 minutes, then pour into hot sterilised jars. Seal when cold.

COOK'S TIP
JAM GEL TEST

Test jam when it has reduced to about half the original quantity of mixture. Remove jam from heat and allow the bubbles to subside. Drop a spoonful onto a chilled saucer, leaving the jam to set at room temperature. Jam should have a skin that will wrinkle when pushed with your finger. If jam is not set sufficiently, return to the heat and boil for a few more minutes and then retest.

❖ LEMON BUTTER

Lemon butter, sometimes called lemon curd or lemon honey, is a firm favourite.

Makes 1 small (185 mL) jar

- ☐ **2 eggs**
- ☐ **¹/₂ cup (125 g) sugar**
- ☐ **grated rind and juice 2 lemons**
- ☐ **30 g butter**

1   Combine eggs and sugar in a heatproof bowl and lightly beat. Stir in lemon rind, lemon juice and butter.

2   Cook in a bowl over a saucepan of boiling water for about 15 minutes, stirring occasionally until mixture thickens.

3   Pour lemon butter into hot sterilised jars. Seal when cold.

❖ HORSERADISH MUSTARD

The flavour of this mustard will develop if stored for two to three weeks before using.

Makes 1 small (125 mL) jar

- ☐ **3 tablespoons dry mustard**
- ☐ **1 tablespoon horseradish relish**
- ☐ **1 teaspoon salt**
- ☐ **3 tablespoons white wine vinegar**
- ☐ **1 tablespoon olive oil**

Combine mustard, horseradish, salt, vinegar and oil in a bowl and blend together until smooth. Pour into sterilised jars and seal. Store in the refrigerator.

❖ APRICOT JAM

Makes 5 small (250 mL) jars

- ☐ **500 g dried apricots**
- ☐ **1¹/₄ litres water**
- ☐ **1 kg sugar**
- ☐ **few drops almond essence**

1   Combine apricots and water in a large bowl. Cover and stand overnight. Transfer apricots and water to a large saucepan. Cook over medium heat for 10 minutes or until apricots are soft.

2   Add sugar and stir until sugar dissolves. Reduce heat and simmer without stirring for 1 hour or until jam gels when tested. Stir in a few drops almond essence, pour into hot sterilised jars and seal when cold.

❖ PORK PIES

Makes 6 pies

FILLING
- ☐ **425 g lean pork fillet, minced**
- ☐ **1 cup (60 g) fresh breadcrumbs**
- ☐ **1 small onion, grated**
- ☐ **¹/₂ teaspoon ground coriander**
- ☐ **¹/₄ teaspoon ground nutmeg**
- ☐ **¹/₂ teaspoon ground thyme**
- ☐ **¹/₄ teaspoon ground sage**
- ☐ **1 egg, beaten**
- ☐ **2 tablespoons milk**

PASTRY
- ☐ **4 cups (500 g) plain flour, sifted**
- ☐ **1 tablespoon baking powder**
- ☐ **250 g lard, chopped**
- ☐ **about 1¹/₂ cups boiling water**
- ☐ **1 egg, beaten**

1 To make filling, place pork, breadcrumbs, onion, coriander, nutmeg, thyme and sage in a mixing bowl. Stir in egg and milk, mixing well to combine.

2 To make pastry, combine flour and baking powder in a bowl. Cut in lard until mixture resembles fine breadcrumbs. Add sufficient boiling water to form a stiff dough. Cover and rest for 30 minutes.

3 Divide pastry into two portions, one portion two-thirds larger than the other. Roll the larger portion out to 3 mm thickness then cut six 15 cm circles (using a saucer as a guide). Line greased ramekins with pastry circles and spoon in filling.

4 Roll remaining pastry to ¹/₄ cm thickness and cut six 8 cm circles. Brush the rim of each pastry case with a little water and top with pastry circles.

5 Crimp edes of pastry to seal and cut steam vents in tops. Brush with beaten egg and bake at 200°C for 40 minutes or until golden brown.

Pork Pies

Cut 15 cm circles.

Crimp edges of pastry to seal.

Chicken Liver Pate, Salmon Pate

❖ CHICKEN LIVER PATE

Makes 4 (185 mL) pate pots

- ☐ **500 g chicken livers, chopped**
- ☐ **4 tablespoons dry sherry**
- ☐ **90 g butter**
- ☐ **2 shallots, chopped**
- ☐ **1 clove garlic, crushed**
- ☐ **4 tablespoons cream**
- ☐ **¹/₄ teaspoon mixed spice**
- ☐ **¹/₂ teaspoon ground thyme**
- ☐ **salt and pepper to taste**
- ☐ **100 g butter, melted**

1 Place livers in a bowl. Cover with sherry and stand for 2 hours. Drain and reserve liquid.

2 Melt half the butter in a frypan. Stir in shallots, garlic and livers. Cook over medium heat for 3 minutes, then pour in reserved liquid and cook for 1 minute more. Remove pan from heat.

3 Place liver mixture in a food processor or blender. Melt remaining butter and combine with cream, mixed spice and thyme, then blend into liver mixture. Season to taste with salt and pepper. Pour pate into individual pate pots, top with melted butter and refrigerate overnight.

❖ SALMON PATE

Makes 4 (185 mL) pate pots

- ☐ **210 g can red salmon, drained**
- ☐ **125 g ricotta cheese**
- ☐ **¹/₂ cup (125 g) mayonnaise**
- ☐ **2 teaspoons grated lemon rind**
- ☐ **2 tablespoons lemon juice**
- ☐ **3 shallots**
- ☐ **125 g butter, melted**

1 Combine salmon, ricotta, mayonnaise, lemon rind, lemon juice and shallots in a food processor. Add butter and process until smooth.

2 Spoon salmon pate into individual pate pots, top with melted butter and refrigerate overnight.

Tea tent treats

Working up an appetite is easy! Make sure no one goes hungry with these tempting ideas for the tea tent, refreshment area or for eating on the go.

❖

SCONES

Makes 24

- ☐ **4 cups (500 g) self-raising flour, sifted**
- ☐ **60 g butter**
- ☐ **2 tablespoons icing sugar**
- ☐ **1¹/₂ cups (375 mL) milk**

1　Place flour in a large mixing bowl. Rub in butter until mixture resembles fine breadcrumbs. Stir in icing sugar, then make a well in centre of dry ingredients and stir in enough milk to give a soft, sticky dough.
2　Turn dough out onto a lightly floured board and knead lightly until smooth. Press dough out to 2 cm thickness and cut into rounds with a 5 cm cutter.
3　Place scones on a greased baking tray. Brush tops with a little milk and bake at 220°C for 12-15 minutes or until golden brown. Stand a few minutes, then place on a wire rack to cool.

COOK'S TIP
THE PERFECT SCONE

1　Scone dough should be soft and sticky, turned out onto a lightly floured surface and kneaded quickly and lightly then pressed out with fingertips.
2　A rolling pin is useful for large quantities of dough. Don't roll too heavily or too thinly. 2 cm is a good thickness.
3　Sugar takes away the floury taste and can be added in any form such as crystal, caster or icing sugar.
4　Add most of the liquid at once and mix only until ingredients are combined. Overmixing will result in heavy, tough scones. The amount of liquid required can alter slightly depending on the quality and age of the flour.
5　Sharp, hollow, metal cutters are best used for scones. Flour the cutters and press straight down into dough. Twisting of the cutters causes dragging on sides of the scones　which will inhibit the raising during cooking.
6　Use a cake pan with 4 cm high sides rather than a scone tray. The sides of the cake pan provide a wall for the scones which prevents them toppling over. Place scones in the greased pan with sides just touching. Overcrowding will prevent the middle scones from cooking evenly.
7　Scones should be cooked at a very high temperature in the middle of the oven. To test if cooked, tap with fingers. They should sound hollow and look evenly browned.
8　Turn scones out on a wire rack to cool. For soft scones, wrap in a clean tea towel or table napkin.
9　To freeze scones, cool completely. Place in a freezer bag. Draw out excess air and seal. Scones can be frozen for up to two months.
10　Reheat frozen scones in the microwave on HIGH (100%) for 1-2 minutes per scone or wrap scones in aluminium foil and warm through in a low oven (150°C).

TEA TENT TIPS

- ❖ Choose food which is simple to cook and eat, for example hamburgers, steak sandwiches, hot dogs, satays and fresh fruit salad.
- ❖ Under-cater rather than over-cater and have food left. If you do have food left over, sell it cheaply at the end of the day.
- ❖ Keep the stall spotlessly clean and maintain good standards of hygiene when handling food.
- ❖ Place a large banner over the stall to attract attention.
- ❖ Keep drinks cool in a portable cooler or fridge.

VARIATIONS

SULTANA SCONES
Add 185 g sultanas to dry ingredients before adding the milk.

DATE SCONES
Add 125 g finely chopped dates to dry ingredients before adding the milk.

❖
FRUIT AND NUT ROLLS

If you do not have a nut roll tin use a washed baked bean or soup tin with both ends removed. Cover the ends with foil.

Makes 2 rolls (15 cm)

- ☐ ²/₃ **cup (120 g) mixed dried fruit**
- ☐ **hot water**
- ☐ **125 g butter**
- ☐ ¹/₂ **cup (85 g) brown sugar**
- ☐ **3 tablespoons golden syrup**
- ☐ **2 eggs**
- ☐ ³/₄ **cup (90 g) plain flour, sifted**
- ☐ **1 cup (125 g) self-raising flour, sifted**
- ☐ **4 tablespoons milk**
- ☐ ¹/₂ **cup (60 g) chopped walnuts**

1   Cover fruit with hot water and stand for 30 minutes. Drain and dry fruit on absorbent paper.
2   Cream butter, sugar and syrup in a small mixing bowl until light and fluffy. Beat in eggs. Combine plain and self-raising flours and fold in alternately with milk. Stir in fruit and walnuts.
3   Spoon mixture evenly into two greased nut roll tins and bake at 180°C for 1 hour. Stand rolls in tin with lids on for 10 minutes. Turn out onto a wire rack to cool.

❖
STRAWBERRY JAM

Remember the easy way to test if jam is set is to drop a spoonful onto a chilled saucer and leave it to set at room temperature. The jam is set when the skin wrinkles if pushed.

Makes 2 small (250 mL) jars

- ☐ **1 kg strawberries, washed and hulled**
- ☐ **1 kg sugar**
- ☐ ¹/₂ **cup (125 mL) lemon juice**
- ☐ ³/₄ **cup (190 mL) water**

1   Combine strawberries, sugar, lemon juice and water in a large saucepan. Cook over medium heat stirring until sugar dissolves.
2   Increase heat and boil without stirring for about 20-25 minutes or until jam gels when tested. Pour jam into hot sterilised jars. Seal when cold.

COOK'S TIP

Be sure not to stir or overmix muffin ingredients after adding the liquid, as this will make the muffins tough and chewy.

❖
BLUEBERRY AND APPLE MUFFINS

If you are unable to find canned blueberries, use frozen ones for these delicious muffins.

Makes 12

- ☐ **3 cups (375 g) self-raising flour, sifted**
- ☐ ¹/₂ **cup (125 g) sugar**
- ☐ **125 g butter**
- ☐ ¹/₂ **cup (100 g) canned apples**
- ☐ ¹/₂ **cup (100 g) canned blueberries, drained**
- ☐ ¹/₂ **cup (125 mL) milk**
- ☐ **2 eggs, lightly beaten**

1   Place flour and sugar in a large mixing bowl. Rub in butter until mixture resembles fine breadcrumbs. Add apples and blueberries to dry ingredients.
2   Combine milk and eggs. Mix into dry ingredients with a fork until just combined. Mixture should be coarse and lumpy.
3   Drop heaped spoonfuls of mixture into well-greased deep muffin or tartlet pans and bake at 220°C for 15-20 minutes until golden brown. Cool on a wire rack.

Plant stall crafts

A plant stall needs early planning to be a success. Include pot-pourri and other scented garden products for variety. They make trustworthy fast sellers at any stall. You need dedicated gardeners or plant lovers in your team from the beginning. This will allow plenty of time for cuttings and divisions to be well rooted. No one wants to buy a plant that is really a leafy stick with no roots. It will be much easier to achieve a professional presentation if you all plan together. There will also be less problems with watering if the pots are evenly filled and potted with a similar mix.

Arrange a meeting well in advance with your team and discuss what each person has growing or what they can acquire. Decide which of these plants are most suitable and reliable for propagation and make notes on what plants you can expect to have. Plants in flower are great for display purposes and much easier to sell. Go for colourful favourites rather than 'interesting' frumps.

Ask for donations of potting mix and small pots (these take less potting mix). Also ask for donations of seedling trays, bulbs, seeds and unwanted plants. Your team will do the planting and repotting.

Arrange a short meeting every month before the big day to allocate donated materials and discuss the planting program. Two weeks before, have a final meeting to discuss transport of plants, signs, stall decorations, naming of plants, labels, pricing and money float.

PRICES

Check local nursery and super-market prices and plan for your plants to be a little cheaper than retail. Prices should be clearly marked. No true gardener can resist a bargain and often a plant bought at a stall is a child's first step into the wonderful world of gardening.

DECORATION

You could plan for a plant theme and decorate the stall accordingly. Where practical, all decorations such as hanging herbs, should also be for sale. Try to arrange for the stall to be large enough to have all plants for sale at eye level. Don't crowd them. Back-up stock should be placed out of harm's way and not where people have to walk over them.

Everything you need for a successful plant stall

Tropical palms and ferns are always popular.

WHAT TO SELL

Tropical plants: Sell ferns, palms, tree ferns, rainforest plants and orchids. Decorate with anything green, such as huge fresh banana leaves, to achieve a luxurious and lush mood. Lightly spray with water during the day to keep everything fresh.

Spring festival: Sell masses of colourful flowering plants such as azaleas, daisies, flowering bulbs, geraniums, primroses, forget-me-nots, Johnny jumpups and violets. Sell cut flowers from brightly coloured plastic buckets. The flowers in bloom will provide most of the display. Decorate with great sprigs of peach or other fruit blossoms.

Fragrant plants: Sell jasmine, Daphne, bulbs in flower, herbs, scented geraniums, lavender, gardenia, heliotrope, lilac, roses and plants with aromatic foliage. Decorate with bunches of lavender and branches of fragrant foliage such as eucalyptus leaves.

Indoor plants: Sell palms, umbrella trees, figs, cyclamens, philodendrons, aspidistras, coleus, dracaenas, asparagus ferns, African violets, begonias, terrarium gardens and ferns. Decorate with hanging baskets or ivy, spider, plant, lipstick plant, grape ivy and Boston fern (also for sale).

Perennials and cottage plants: Sell flowering favourites such as iris, dianthus, lillies, euphorbias, primroses, agapanthus, lavender, daisies, salvias, fuschias, geraniums and roses. Include grey foliage plants. Decorate with garlands of ivy and bunches of red rosehips.

Herbs: Sell all types of herbs including culinary, medicinal, fragrant and those suitable for dyeing. Include hard-to-get and collector varieties. Sell compatible herbs in herb baskets. Decorate with hanging bunches of dried herbs tied with ribbon (also for sale).

Rockery: Sell miniature and small-growing plants, including alpines, ground covers, succulents and cacti. Decorate with large papier-mache rocks made by the children (also for sale).

POTTED PLANTS

Pots: Never pot plants in old rusty tins or plastic containers with permanent labels such as yoghurt or margarine. They look awful. Most sales only last for one day and all the plants need to be sold out by the end of the day. You will be left with all the plants in tacky containers. All used containers should be scrubbed with a brush and a little detergent before being used. This removes any disease and ensures better presentation. Although terracotta containers have a special charm, neat plastic pots will do the job and are lighter to carry. Ensure there are adequate drainage holes in the pots prior to filling.

Colourful flowering plants are certain sellers.

Potting mix: Use only a prepared potting mix. Don't use tired soil from the garden. Make sure the soil in the pots is a reasonably open mixture and remove any grass and other weeds. Top up the soil to within about 2 or 3 cm of the top a few days before the fete.

Watering: Water your plants regularly during growing and on the day before make sure you give them a good watering. Don't try to transport the plants to the stall or sell them dripping wet. Take a watering can along with you on the day only for emergencies.

Labelling: Ideally, all plants should be clearly labelled with the correct botanical name, the common name and the size of the plant. You can buy blank labels and the correct marking pen from a nursery.

Garden herbs in classic terracotta pots

HERB BASKETS

An extremely attractive way to sell herbs grown in containers is in groups presented in baskets. Baskets can be found in a profusion of shapes and sizes. Woven baskets must be lined to retain the soil. Cut the paper bark to the shape of the basket and overlap it so that the soil does not escape while still allowing good water drainage. The soil for baskets must be a well-drained and fairly rich type. Unlike herbs grown in the open garden, container herbs must draw all their nutrients from the small amount of soil in the basket. When you plant several herbs in one container, choose herbs that require similar amounts of water, sun and soil conditions.

Since most herbs are used in the kitchen, the popular choice for a herb basket would be a selection of culinary herbs, such as basil, thyme, chives, coriander, marjoram, parsley, sage or tarragon.

As mints prefer more moisture and are inclined to take over other herbs, a separate basket containing a combination of mints is a good idea.

A herbal tea basket could contain chamomile, lemon balm, valerian, peppermint or lemon verbena.

Dried sweet-smelling ingredients create delightful potpourri.

❖
PERFUMED GARDEN

The secret of a successful potpourri, sachet mix and dried herbs for culinary and cosmetic purposes lies in the drying process. All ingredients, except for the essential oils, must be thoroughly and quickly dried so that optimum fragrance and colour is retained. Any material that has a hint of moisture should be discarded as this could turn the whole batch mouldy. Spices will help the potpourri hold its scent and add a special fragrance to it. Spices must be fresh and coarsely ground as needed.

FIXATIVES

Fixatives are essential to help fix and stabilise the overall perfume for a very long time. The most common fixative is orris root powder which slows the evaporation of the oils. When dried, orris root powder has a delicate violet scent. Other fixatives include gum benzoin, sandalwood and oakmoss. Dried citrus rinds such as orange and lemon peel are also good for fixing a scent. The rinds must be pared very thinly from the fruit to avoid leaving any pith attached which can send the peel mouldy.

ESSENTIAL OILS

Essential oils enhance the scent of most potpourri and sachet blends, but should be used very sparingly. Add one drop at a time, smelling and blending as you go. Fixatives and essential oils can be obtained from a chemist or health food shop.

POTPOURRI

The best containers to sell potpourri in are transparent because they enable you to show off the colours. Collect attractive glass jars with lids and celluloid boxes of different shapes. If you have a lot of potpourri to package, fill cellophane confectionery bags and tie with a ribbon. Specially made pottery potpourri containers with cork stoppers are also popular.

The following recipes are only a guide to different styles of potpourri you can make. Adapt them to the plant material you have available. Ingredients can be doubled for a larger mix, but always be cautious when adding essential oils.

Step by step

1 Place all dried flowers in a large bowl and add the dry fixatives.
2 Add spices and herbs to further enhance the scent. Toss to mix thoroughly.
3 If you want a stronger scent, you may add an essential oil. The more oil you add, the stronger the scent will be. Use an eye dropper for better distribution.
4 After adding oils, mix your potpourri well with your hands. Pour into a large container and seal. Leave to mature for around six weeks.
5 When aged, transfer to containers for selling and decorate with colourful or pressed flowers and ferns.

❖
FRENCH COUNTRY POTPOURRI

- ☐ **4 cups red rose petals**
- ☐ **1 cup lavender flowers**
- ☐ **1 cup each rosemary, thyme, sage and marjoram**
- ☐ **2 tablespoons coriander seeds, lightly crushed**
- ☐ **¹⁄₂ cup dried lemon peel**
- ☐ **1 cup fixative**
- ☐ **6-8 drops rose oil**
- ☐ **3-4 drops lavender oil**

Dried whole cornflowers, red roses and lavender spikes for decoration

❖
CITRUS POTPOURRI

- ☐ **8 cups of a combination of any or all of the following: lemon verbena, lemon-scented tea tree, lemon thyme, lemon-scented geranium and/or lemon grass**
- ☐ **1 cup eau-de-cologne mint**
- ☐ **1 cup calendula petals**
- ☐ **¹/₂ cup each orange and lemon peel**
- ☐ **1 cup whole allspice, lightly crushed**
- ☐ **1 cup fixative**
- ☐ **6-8 drops lemon verbena oil**
- ☐ **3-4 drops bergamot oil**

Dried daffodils, nasturtiums, everlasting daisies or pressed wattle sprigs for decoration.

❖
WOODY POTPOURRI

- ☐ **8 cups aromatic foliage which might include eucalyptus leaves, rosemary, scented geraniums, bay leaves, basil, lavender foliage**
- ☐ **2 cups sandalwood chips, cedar chips or pine shavings**
- ☐ **1 cup cinnamon sticks, broken into chunky bits**
- ☐ **1 cup whole coriander seeds or juniper berries, lightly bruised**

❖
AROMATIC BATH OILS

If you have a lot of flowers and herbs you can make aromatic bath oils.

Use strongly-scented flowers like:
- ☐ **roses**
- ☐ **lavender**

and therapeutic herbs:
- ☐ **rosemary**
- ☐ **lemon verbena**
- ☐ **chamomile**
- ☐ **mint**
- ☐ **thyme**

1   Pour 6 cups of light, non-smelling oil into a large bowl. Add as many flowers or herbs as the bowl will hold and saturate the petals or leaves.

2   Allow to soak for 24 hours.

3   Remove flowers or herbs with slotted spoon and discard. Add more fresh flowers or herbs to oil.

4   Repeat with six batches of flowers or herbs, then strain liquid through cheesecloth.

Gourmet herb oils and vinegars

5   Transfer oil to attractive bottles and cap tightly.

DRIED HERBS

Dried herbs can be sold in separate cellophane bags for use in the kitchen and bathroom, and for making teas.

Culinary: Those that retain their flavour best when dried include rosemary, thyme, mint, oregano, marjoram, and bay leaves.

Herbal teas: Popular herbs for teas include chamomile, lemon grass, peppermint and a rose petal and lemon verbena blend.

Hair rinses: Herbal hair rinses are used as a final rinse after washing the hair. Boil a handful of herbs for 20 minutes and strain. Use chamomile for blondes and rosemary for dark-haired people.

❖
HERB VINEGARS

Flavoured vinegar can give extra flavour to any savoury dish, pickle or salad that normally calls for vinegar in the recipe.

1   Wash herbs gently, shake and pat dry thoroughly.

2   2 cups of slightly crushed fresh herb leaves to every litre of vinegar.

3   Pour the vinegar over the herbs, seal and leave for about one week.

4   Strain the liquid and discard the herbs.

5   Repeat the process using fresh leaves and leave again for another week.

6   Strain the vinegar into sterilised jars, decorate with a whole sprig or two of the herb used and label.

Scented sachets filled with lavender and potpourri

Packaging & presentation

Attractive packaging will make a big difference to how your goodies sell on the day. We have a feast of practical and fun presentation ideas here – colourful ribbons, lots of clear cellophane and different textures and fabrics.

Use attractive swing labels to identify your sweets and wrap them in clear cellophane – it's the best way to tempt a prospective buyer! Remember your sweets and cakes must be stored at the appropriate temperature. Package up fudge and rocky roads before the big day but make sure they don't sweat and become moist. Transparent coverings are also a good idea for specialty items like handmade soaps, giving them a natural, unfettered look. For other goods, like bouquet garni, keep muslin bags spotlessly clean and use coloured embroidery string to tie them. Line some little boxes and bowls with pretty print fabric, fill them with the bouquet garni and arrange them around your stall.

Make the most of your toffee apples' glossy toffee coating by wrapping them in clear cellophane – bunch the cellophane around the wooden sticks and tie it with pretty ribbons.

For herb oils and vinegars, use bottles of all different shapes and sizes – and seal them with a cork so they really look the part. Place a sprig of the appropriate herb in the bottle for decoration.

Uniformly shaped packages like our sewing cases and covered picture frames are easy to wrap so set up a production line of volunteers to get it all done in a jiffy! Use generous amounts of clear cellophane to show off items.

Show off the colours and textures of your gourmet jams and relishes with plain jars topped with pretty country-style gingham and lace covers. Ask a helper with neat handwriting to identify each using stick-on labels – if you can, use decorative labels as we have. Complete the effect with beautiful curling ribbons in complementary colours. Sundry items such as wine, individually wrapped sweets and gourmet goods look wonderful presented in a basket. Line your basket with clear cellophane or tissue paper, wind fabric or florist's ribbon around the handle and base, and use it as the centrepiece to your stall.

Collect traditional white boxes or ones with patterns as we have here. Tie the box with curling ribbon or select a colour to complement the cake's decoration. Display a piece of cake when using packaging such as this so people can see what they are buying. When using clear cellophane to present your cakes, place toothpicks in the cake top to hold the wrapping away from the icing, gather at the top and secure with some ribbon and a swing ticket.

Craft stall creations

No market or bazaar would be complete without a craft stall, laden with wonderful handmade items from traditional coat hangers and pot holders to the more exotic covered photograph frames and stencilled flower press.

Start planning your craft stall as early as you can. Unlike cakes and sweets, craft items can be made many months in advance and stored quite easily. Call a meeting of all those interested in contributing to a craft stall. Members of your team may have special talents, such as painting sun hats or making lavender sachets and will be happy to make a number of these for the stall, but others will require some inspiration and direction.

You will have to make decisions about whether to 'buy or beg' the necessary materials for each project. Make lists of all the materials you will need including fabrics, ribbons, lace, baskets, boxes and so on.

Once you know who can do what, draw up a list of items to be made, taking into account all the skills you have at your disposal, and making sure there is something for everyone who wants to participate. There will be many simple tasks for willing hands and the more of those you have the better! Make up a master plan and give all the team members a copy with their own project highlighted. You should also prepare copies of patterns and instructions and lists of all materials required and where

they can be obtained.

The master plan should also indicate a timetable for the work to be done and a projected collection day. Don't leave this too late as unforeseen problems could leave you short of craft items to sell with no time to make up the difference. The schedule should give you plenty of time to check, wrap and price.

Most of us love a little company while we work and a sewing day is a great way to share skills and ideas around the group.

PRICES

The price should reflect the cost, work and care that has gone into making the item but still be below the price charged for something similar in a shop. Each item should be clearly priced, perhaps using attractive swing tickets.

DECORATION

Decorated baskets make wonderful containers for small items. Cover the counter with a pretty fabric or some firm paper. Don't crowd the stall but keep extras in covered boxes under the counter.

A collection of crafty creations to make

❖ FLOWER PRESS

- ☐ **two pieces of plywood, each 18 cm x 18 cm and 1 cm thick**
- ☐ **four 5 cm bolts**
- ☐ **four butterfly nuts and four washers to fit bolts**
- ☐ **cardboard like that used for cartons**
- ☐ **sheets of blotting paper**
- ☐ **stencilling equipment**

1 Round off corners of plywood and paint in preferred colour.
2 Stencil motif onto one piece of plywood following How to Stencil instructions.
3 Mark and drill holes for bolts at each corner of plywood pieces, taking care to align holes in top and lower pieces.
4 Cut several sheets of cardboard and blotting paper each 18 cm square. Cut off corners to allow for bolts.
5 Insert bolts through unstencilled piece of plywood. Layer sheets of cardboard and blotting paper on top of plywood. Place stencilled plywood over cardboard, passing bolts through holes.
6 Attach washers and butterfly nuts.

To use press, lay your chosen flowers onto blotting paper, cover with another sheet of blotting paper and then a sheet of cardboard. Continue to assemble layers in this fashion. Close press, tightening nuts, and place in a cool, dry place. Open press after about three weeks to check on progress. If flowers are completely dry and papery to the touch they are ready to remove from press.

❖ MUSHROOM BAG

- ☐ **stencilling equipment**
- ☐ **piece calico 50 cm x 40 cm**
- ☐ **90 cm of 1.5 cm wide twill tape**

1 Make stencil and stencil motif onto front of bag following How to Stencil instructions.
2 Fold calico over double, with right sides facing and 40 cm sides matching. Stitch sides.
3 Turn in 6 mm at top raw edge and again 5 cm. Stitch.
4 Stitch centre of tape to one side of bag, sewing in small box shape.

❖ SUN HAT

- ☐ **wide-brimmed straw hat**
- ☐ **stencilling equipment**

1 Make stencil of roses and leaves as described in How to Stencil.
2 Stencil roses and leaves around hat brim as shown.

❖ PLANT POTS

- ☐ **terracotta pots**
- ☐ **stencilling equipment**

1 Make stencil as instructed in How to Stencil.
2 Stencil motif around pots.
3 Using stencil paints, decorate pots with bows and four-petalled small flowers.

❖ TEDDY BEAR CUSHION

- ☐ **stencilling equipment**
- ☐ **piece calico 42 cm x 42 cm**
- ☐ **two pieces backing fabric, each 22 cm x 42 cm**
- ☐ **40 cm polyester cushion insert**
- ☐ **3.2 m of 12 cm wide strips backing fabric for ruffles**
- ☐ **3.2 m of 2.5 cm wide lace**
- ☐ **two small shirt buttons**
- ☐ **30 cm zipper**

1 One cm allowed for all seams. Join strips to form a continuous circle. Fold over double with wrong sides together. Press. Attach lace to folded edge. Gather raw edges to length required to go around cushion.
2 Stencil motif onto calico, following How to Stencil instructions.
3 Sew ruffle around edge of stencilled calico, with right sides together and raw edges even.
4 Sew ends of cushion back centre seam, leaving opening for zipper.
5 Insert zipper.
6 Place cushion front and cushion back together with right sides facing. Sew around edges through all thicknesses. Turn cushion through zipper opening.
7 Sew two shirt buttons below Teddy's bow tie.

> *Note: See stencil templates, pages 46-47.*

How To STENCIL

- ☐ **firm plastic for cutting stencils**
- ☐ **stencil brushes**
- ☐ **paints**
- ☐ **felt-tipped pen**
- ☐ **craft knife**
- ☐ **bread board or similar cutting surface**

1 Place plastic over stencil design. Trace around each section of the same colour. Make a separate stencil for each colour. To test that you have traced design completely, place all the plastic sheets together and you should see the whole motif.
2 Cut out outlined sections.
3 Decide where you want your motif to fall and place largest piece first.
4 Painting with flat surface of brush, carefully fill in colour, using light dabbing motions rather than strokes. Do not use too much paint at a time and have a separate brush for each colour. Practise stencilling on scraps until pleased with your results.
5 Stencil in each design element until motif is complete.
6 Wash stencils thoroughly after use and store for use another time.

Inset: A useful bag for refrigerating mushrooms

Stencilling adds a finishing touch.

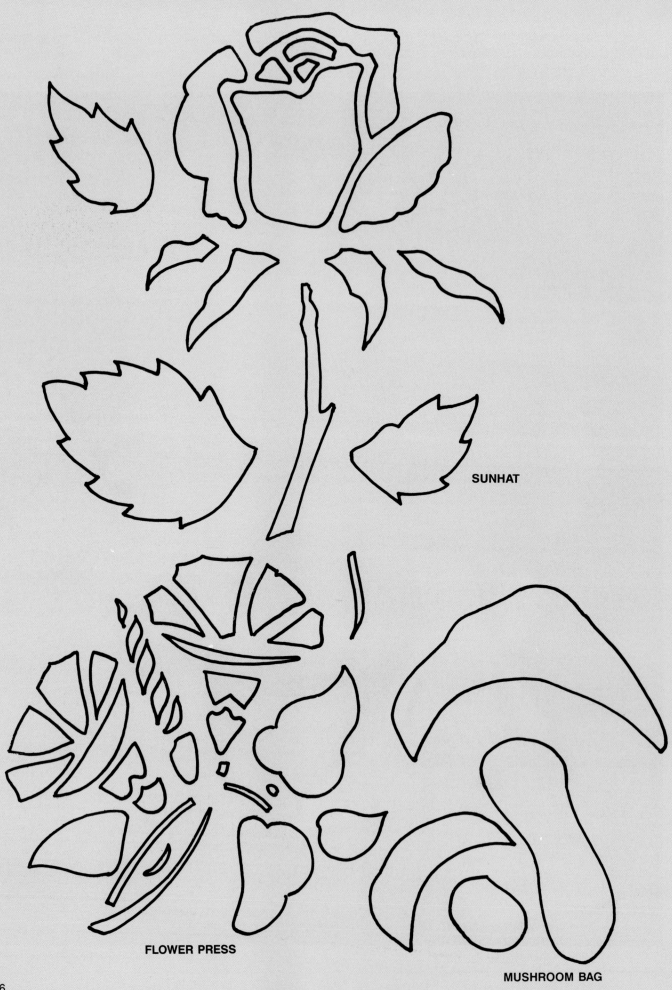

SUNHAT

FLOWER PRESS

MUSHROOM BAG

46

TEDDY BEAR CUSHION

POT PLANT

MUSHROOM BAG

❖
FABRIC-COVERED PICTURE FRAMES

- ☐ **pieces strong cardboard in desired size**
- ☐ **pieces fabric and wadding in desired size**
- ☐ **clear craft glue or spray-on photographic glue**
- ☐ **strong scissors**
- ☐ **craft knife**
- ☐ **cutting board**
- ☐ **lace, bows and ribbons for trimming**

1   Cut out three shapes from cardboard – one for backing, one for centre piece and one which will have centre cut out to reveal picture. Cut a piece of cardboard for stand approximately 5 cm x 10 cm.

2   Cover one side of backing piece with glue. Apply wadding to this side. Trim wadding to within 1 cm of cardboard. Turn 1 cm to other side, clipping curves and excess wadding at corners. Glue into place. Cover with fabric in same way.

3   Cover one side of centre piece with fabric in same way, omitting wadding.

4   Cut out centre of front section. Cover with glue, wadding and fabric as for backing. Take care to clip curves so that wadding and fabric will turn to wrong side without too much bulk.

5   Glue centre and backing pieces together with fabric sides outwards. Glue front section onto completed backing, with fabric side outwards and leaving top section unglued to allow picture to be inserted.

6   Cover stand with wadding and fabric. Bend 1.5 cm at one end of stand. Glue this end to back of frame at a point which allows frame to stand properly. You may wish to add a length of ribbon between stand and frame for added stability.

Trimming notes: Take care when placing fabric to take best advantage of print. Pre-gathered lace is easier to use for trimming than flat lace.

Note: See patterns, pages 58-59.

HOW TO MAKE
RIBBON ROSES

- ☐ **satin or nylon ribbon of desired width (the wider the ribbon the larger the rose will be)**
- ☐ **stem wire**
- ☐ **26 gauge florist's wire or fine fuse wire**
- ☐ **green florist's winding tape**

1   Bend one end of stem wire over to form a hook. Secure with fine wire (A).

2   Fasten end of ribbon around hook with fine wire (B).

3   Fold ribbon over hook (C) and continue winding it to form bud, securing it with fine wire (D).

4   To make petals, hold stem in one hand and fold ribbon towards you (E). The fold forms top of petal.

5   Turn stem anti-clockwise, winding ribbon onto bud as you turn. As ribbon straightens out after each fold make another diagonal fold as before (F). Bind end of rose with fine wire.

6   Gather end of ribbon at base of rose. Secure with wire (G).

7   Cover base of rose by twisting green florist's tape around it.

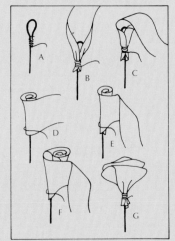

❖ PINCUSHION

- [ ] **small tin, about 8-10 cm high, empty and thoroughly cleaned**
- [ ] **polyester wadding or cotton wool**
- [ ] **remnant pretty cotton print fabric**
- [ ] **about 30 cm gathered eyelet lace**
- [ ] **satin ribbon to fit eyelets and 3 mm wide ribbon for trimming**
- [ ] **clear-drying craft glue**
- [ ] **pearl-headed pins**

1 Cut out a circle of fabric large enough to cover tin and a strip of wadding to go around outside of tin. Glue wadding into place. Place tin in centre of fabric and draw fabric up sides. Push top edge of fabric into tin and secure with glue. Fill tin with wadding so that wadding protrudes at top.

2 Cut out a circle of fabric large enough to cover top of tin. Place fabric over top of tin. Glue it into place around side of tin, folding raw edge under as you go.

3 Thread ribbon through eyelet lace. Glue lace around tin, covering fabric edge.

4 Make several bows out of 3 mm wide ribbon and attach over ends of lace.

❖ PINE CONE PINCUSHION

- [ ] **open pine cone**
- [ ] **scraps co-ordinating cotton print fabric**
- [ ] **cotton wool balls or polyester fibre**
- [ ] **clear-drying craft glue**

Pretty picture frames are always popular.

1 Cut out squares of fabric large enough to cover a cotton wool ball. Place one ball into each square, drawing up fabric corners to enclose ball. Wind thread around to secure. Trim away excess fabric.

2 Place a drop of glue into each opening in pine cone.

3 Using a screwdriver, push each small cushion into pine cone.

4 Decorate with ribbon bows.

❖ HAIRBANDS, BANGLES AND COMBS

- [ ] **inexpensive plastic hairband, comb or bangle**
- [ ] **1 cm wide satin or nylon ribbon and 3 mm wide matching ribbon**
- [ ] **clear-drying craft glue**
- [ ] **several green silk leaves**
- [ ] **ribbon roses to match or contrast**
- [ ] **green florist's winding tape**

HAIRBANDS

1 Make several bows out of narrow ribbon. Glue or tie to centre of hairband.

2 Tie approximately 60 cm of narrow ribbon around centre of hairband, over centre of bows, allowing ends to fall loosely. If you have a microwave oven you can curl the ribbon, as we have done for the blue band, by winding approximately 90 cm of slightly damp narrow ribbon around a plastic cotton reel. Place it in your microwave for approximately 30 seconds. Allow to cool then unwind. The lilac band has no fall of ribbons.

3 Glue silk leaves on either side of bows.

4 Make ribbon roses and glue to band between bow loops.

5 For lilac band, place bows slightly to one side and glue leaves on either side of bows. Attach ribbon roses between bow loops.

BANGLES

1 Wind 1 cm wide ribbon around bangle to cover it completely. Glue ends into place.

2 Make ribbon loops as for hairbands and tie into place.

3 Glue on leaves and ribbon roses.

COMBS

1 Make ribbon rosebuds on wire stems. Cover stems with green winding tape. Glue on to comb with green silk leaves.

2 Make ribbon roses and glue to centre of comb over leaves.

❖
HAIR RIBBON HOLDER

- [ ] **two pieces pretty cotton print fabric, 35 cm x 12 cm and 60 cm x 4 cm**
- [ ] **lightweight wadding 35 cm x 36 cm**
- [ ] **about 70 cm ungathered lace or 36 cm gathered lace**
- [ ] **about 30 cm of 12 mm wide elastic**
- [ ] **1.5 m of 12 mm wide satin ribbon**
- [ ] **32 cm ruler**

1   Wrap ruler tightly with wadding, folding in ends and stitching to secure.
2   Gather lace and sew to right side of one long edge of 35 cm x 12 cm fabric.
3   Press in 1 cm at ends of fabric. Fold fabric over wadding-covered ruler, bringing long sides of fabric together. Fold in raw edge of untrimmed side and handsew to lace-trimmed edge.
4   Fold long strip of fabric over double with right sides facing. Stitch long side, turn and press. Insert elastic and attach to one end. Pull up elastic, ruffling fabric as you go. Secure other end.
5   Place ends of elastic piece between folded edges of fabric covering ruler. Handsew into place, closing ends.
6   Fold ends of 1 m satin ribbon into small loops. Stitch each loop to one end of ruler. Cover stitching with small bow at each end. Attach another bow at centre of hanging loop.

❖
GATHERED
COAT HANGER

- [ ] **strip cotton fabric, 15 cm x length of coat hanger plus 25 cm**
- [ ] **small bias strip fabric or ribbon to cover hook**
- [ ] **ribbon for trimming**
- [ ] **polyester wadding**
- [ ] **wooden coat hanger**

1   Cut strips of wadding about 5 cm wide and wind around wood. Stitch ends to secure.
2   Fold fabric double lengthways, with right sides facing and raw edges even. Stitch long and one short side. Turn.
3   Stitch a gathering thread along both long sides. Slide cover onto hanger. Pull up gathering to fit. Stitch open end closed by hand.
4   Fold bias strip over double lengthways

with right sides together. Stitch long and one short side. Turn to right side. Slide over hook. Handsew to secure. Alternatively, wind ribbon around to conceal hook. Insert hook into hanger through all thicknesses of fabric.
5   Trim hanger with bow.

❖
COAT HANGER WITH
GATHERED TOP

- [ ] **20 cm of 115 cm wide fabric**
- [ ] **polyester wadding**
- [ ] **small bias strip of fabric or ribbon to cover hook**
- [ ] **ribbon for trimming**
- [ ] **wooden coat hanger**

1   Cut two pieces of fabric each 38 cm x 9 cm for top of hanger and two pieces 23 cm x 9 cm for lower pieces. Round off one end of all pieces uniformly. Cover is made for each end separately, then joined in the middle.
2   Cut wadding into 5 cm wide strips and wind around wood. Handsew ends to secure.
3   Gather long sides and around curved end of top sections. Draw up gathering to fit length of lower pieces.
4   Stitch upper and lower sections together, with right sides facing and raw edges even, leaving straight ends open. Turn. Slide both sections onto hanger, turning in raw edges at centre. Handsew sections together at centre.
5   Fold bias strip over double with right sides facing. Stitch long and one short side. Turn. Slide over hook. Alternatively wind ribbon around hook to conceal. Insert hook into hanger and handsew bias or ribbon to secure.
6   Tie ribbon around hanger to conceal stitching. Tie bow around hook.

❖
FLAT COAT HANGER
COVER

- [ ] **strip cotton fabric, approximately 40 cm x 50 cm**
- [ ] **lace and ribbon for trimming**
- [ ] **bias strip or ribbon to cover hook**
- [ ] **polyester wadding**
- [ ] **wooden coat hanger**

1   Cut wadding into 5 cm wide strips and wind around wood. Handsew to secure.
2   Place wrapped wood on top of double

layer of fabric. Draw 1¹/₂ cm from shape of top curve and ends of hanger. Continue drawing rest of cover shape to measure 11 cm from centre of hanger. Cut out.

3 Place cover sections together, with right sides facing and raw edges even. Sew around curved edge, leaving small break in stitching for inserting hook.

4 Turn in 6 mm at lower edge and again 6 mm. Stitch. Trim with lace.

5 Fold bias strip over double lengthways, with right sides facing and raw edges even. Stitch long and one short side. Turn. Slide over hook. Alternatively wind ribbon around hook to conceal.

6 Slip cover over hanger. Insert hook and handsew bias or ribbon to secure.

7 Trim hanger with ribbon.

❖

SCENTED SHOE STUFFERS

☐ **20 cm of 115 cm wide cotton fabric**
☐ **polyester stuffing, lavender or potpourri**
☐ **lace and ribbon for trimming**

1 Cut four shapes from fabric. With right sides facing and raw edges even, stitch pairs together around curved edge. Clip seams. Turn and press.

2 Turn under 4 mm at raw edge and again 6 mm. Stitch. Trim with lace if desired.

3 Fill shoe stuffers as desired. Tie bows made from ribbon or self-fabric bias around tops to secure.

Note: See pattern, page 78.

Left: A basketful of handmade coat hangers, ribbon holder and scented shoe stuffers

Sweet teddy bears and mouse to sew

TEDDY BEAR

- ☐ **20 cm of 115 cm wide cotton fabric**
- ☐ **polyester fibre for stuffing**
- ☐ **two small beads for eyes**
- ☐ **embroidery thread**

1 Cut out pattern pieces as directed. All pieces will be joined with right sides facing. Clip all curved seams for ease.

2 Sew pairs of arm and leg pieces together, leaving upper straight edge open. Turn and stuff firmly.

3 Sew pairs of body pieces together along one curved edge. Sew these segments together to form body shape, leaving upper straight edge open. Turn and stuff firmly.

4 Sew pairs of ear pieces together around curved edge. Turn. Turn in 6 mm on open raw edge. Stuff lightly.

5 Sew head centre back and centre front seams. Join front and back head sections. Clip seam, turn and stuff firmly.

6 Using thread doubled, sew a gathering thread around open edge of each body piece. Pull up gathering to close. Secure. Sew arms, legs and head to body. Legs may be attached in either sitting or standing position. Sew ears to head.

7 Embroider nose and mouth. Sew on beads for eyes.

8 To complete your bear, add a bow around its neck or a row of gathered lace. A trimmed straw hat is a sweet touch.

MOUSE

- ☐ **15 cm of 115 cm wide cotton fabric**
- ☐ **small piece iron-on interfacing**
- ☐ **polyester stuffing**
- ☐ **two small beads for eyes**
- ☐ **buttonhole thread or dental floss for whiskers**
- ☐ **3 mm wide satin ribbon**

1 Cut out pattern pieces as directed.

2 Interface ear pieces. Place ear pieces together, in pairs, with right sides facing. Stitch around curved edge. Clip seams, turn and press. Turn in 6 mm at open raw edge. Press.

3 Place long raw edges of tail together with right sides of fabric facing. Stitch, leaving straight edge open for turning. Turn and stuff firmly.

4 Make darts in body pieces. Place body pieces together with right sides facing. Stitch around from A to B, leaving opening for stuffing and attaching tail. Stuff body. Tuck tail into opening and handsew into place, closing opening as you go.

5 Make 1 cm pleat in each ear. Attach ears to head.

6 Sew on eyes.

7 Stitch through snout with several strands of buttonhole thread or dental floss. Clip to form whiskers.

8 Tie bow around neck.

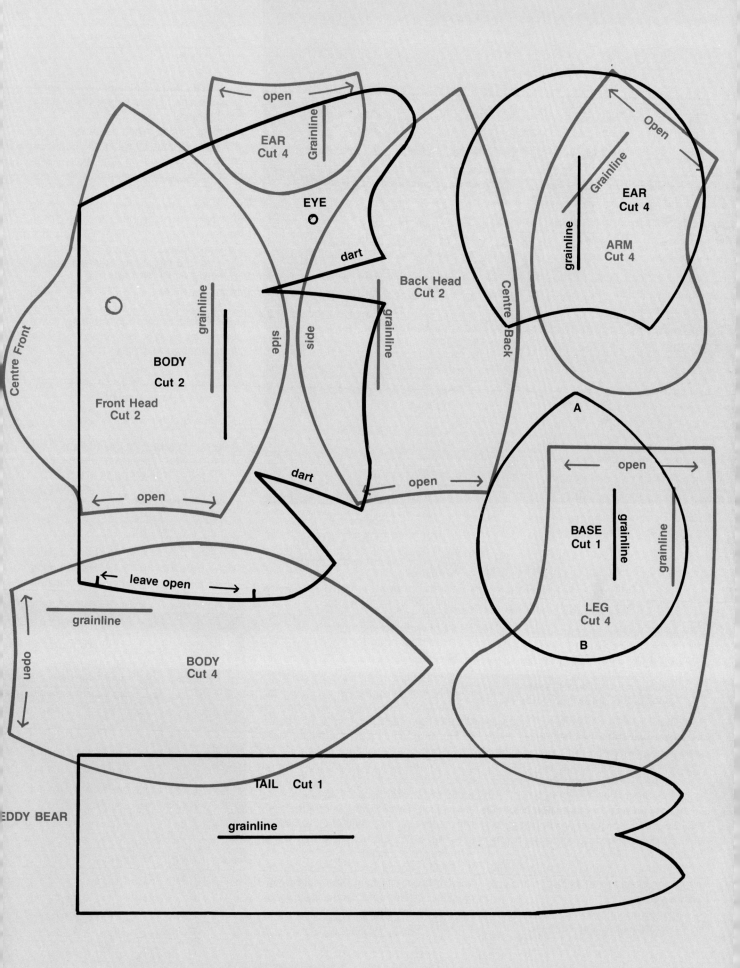

EAR
Cut 4

EYE

open

Grainline

dart

Back Head
Cut 2

grainline

side

side

grainline

Centre Front

BODY
Cut 2

Front Head
Cut 2

grainline

open

dart

open

Open

Grainline

grainline

EAR
Cut 4

ARM
Cut 4

Centre Back

A

open

grainline

grainline

BASE
Cut 1

LEG
Cut 4

B

leave open

grainline

open

BODY
Cut 4

TAIL   Cut 1

grainline

TEDDY BEAR

MOUSE

Egg basket cover, oven mitt and pot holder for that kitchen tea gift

❖ SEWING KIT

☐ two rectangles double-sided quilted fabric, one 15 cm x 22 cm, the other 15 cm x 10 cm
☐ 1.2 m bias binding
☐ needles, pins, scissors, tape measure and threads to equip kit

1 Bind one 15 cm edge of smaller rectangle with bias binding. Place this piece on larger piece, with wrong sides together and raw edges matching. Pin into place. Round off all corners. Stitch around edge, securing pocket.

2 Fold two 18 cm lengths of bias binding over double. Stitch. Knot one end of each strip. Stitch other ends to inside centre top and bottom of kit as shown.

3 Bind all around edge of sewing kit with remaining bias binding, encasing ends of ties as you go.

4 Stitch down centre of pocket, through all thicknesses, dividing it into two.

❖ EGG BASKET COVER

☐ 40 cm of 115 cm wide cotton fabric
☐ scrap contrasting cotton for comb and underside of wings
☐ 40 cm x 80 cm iron-on interfacing
☐ 1 cm wide elastic
☐ open basket about 18 cm in diameter

1 Cut two chickens each from main fabric and interfacing. Cut two wings each from main fabric, contrast fabric and interfacing. Cut two beaks and two combs each from contrasting fabric and interfacing. Iron interfacing onto all pattern pieces.

2 Place main and contrast fabric wings together with wrong sides facing. Stitch all around 6 mm from edge. Trim fabric close to stitching. Stitch again all around edge with satin stitch, covering previous stitching. Stitch feather lines onto wings with straight stitching.

3 Stitch around wing openings. Trim fabric close to stitching. Satin stitch over previous stitching as for wings. Stitch wings onto chicken above openings, along marked lines.

4 Place beak sections and comb sections together with wrong sides facing. Stitch around edges. Trim fabric close to stitching. Satin stitch around edges, covering previous stitching. Pin beak and comb into position on right side of one chicken body piece, keeping raw edges even.

5 Place two chicken body pieces together with right sides facing. Stitch, leaving lower edge open. Clip seams. Turn and press.

6 Turn in 6 mm along raw lower edge. Turn in another 1.5 cm. Stitch to form casing, leaving opening for elastic. Thread elastic through. Place cover on basket to adjust elastic. Secure ends of elastic. Close opening by hand.

Note: See pattern, page 78.

❖ OVEN MITT

☐ piece quilted cotton 30 cm x 40 cm
☐ contrast fabric 20 cm x 20 cm
☐ strip second contrast fabric 5 cm x 37 cm, or a length of braid
☐ 10 cm bias binding or fabric strip for hanging loop

1 Cut two mitt shapes and two contrast bands. With raw edges matching and with right side of bands facing wrong side of mitts, stitch bands to mitts. Press bands to right side. Trim raw edge with second

contrast strip or braid. Neaten any raw edges and stitch down.

2 Make loop of bias binding and attach to corner of right side of one mitt section with raw edges even.

3 Place two mitt shapes together with right sides facing. Stitch around edge, reinforcing stitching at fork of thumb and finger. Clip seam for ease. Turn and press. **Note: See pattern, page 78.**

❖
POT HOLDER

- ☐ **piece quilted fabric 40 cm x 74 cm**
- ☐ **two pieces contrast fabric, each 22 cm x 20 cm**
- ☐ **40 cm strip second contrasting fabric or braid**

1 Cut quilted fabric in half lengthways so that each piece is 20 cm x 74 cm.

2 Trim one 20 cm end of each contrast strip with second contrast or braid, enclosing raw edge.

3 Place quilted fabric pieces and contrast pieces together. Round off all corners. Place contrast pieces on each end of one quilted section so that wrong side of contrast piece faces right side of quilted piece. Place other quilted piece on top so that right sides of quilted pieces are facing. Stitch all around, leaving a small opening for turning near centre. Clip seam. Turn and press. Close opening by hand.

Above: Shower cap, toiletry bag and toilet roll holder are pretty bathroom accessories.

❖
SHOWER CAP

- ☐ **60 cm each of 115 cm wide cotton fabric and plastic sheeting**
- ☐ **twice 2 m bias binding (one could be self fabric)**
- ☐ **1 cm wide elastic**

1 Cut circles 60 cm in diameter from fabric and plastic.

2 Place plastic against wrong side of fabric. Stitch around outside edge. Trim close to stitching.

3 Bind edge with bias binding. Stitch second length of bias binding around inside, 6 cm from edge, to form casing for elastic.

4 Insert elastic. Check fit. Secure ends of elastic.

Left: Simple to sew sewing kit

❖
TOILETRY BAG

- ☐ **pieces cotton fabric and plastic sheeting, each 60 cm x 28 cm**
- ☐ **1.6 m of 12 mm wide satin ribbon**

1 Fold fabric over double lengthways, with right sides together. Stitch sides. Repeat for plastic.

2 Turn fabric bag right side out. Trim 5 cm from top of plastic bag. Slip plastic bag inside fabric bag.

3 Turn in 6 mm at top edge of fabric bag. Turn another 5 cm to cover edge of plastic bag. Stitch through all thicknesses along fold and again 1.5 cm away to form casing.

4 Open stitching of fabric side seams between casing lines. Cut length of ribbon in half Thread half in through one opening, through casing and out same opening. Repeat with other ribbon at other opening.

5 Knot ends of ribbon together.

❖
PLACEMATS WITH CONTRAST CENTRES

These two placemats are made following the same basic instructions but one has a single piece contrast centre while the other has a contrast panel made from strips of co-ordinating contrast fabrics.

- ☐ **piece cotton fabric 50 cm x 64 cm**
- ☐ **piece fine wadding 36 cm x 64 cm**
- ☐ **centre panel 40 cm x 26 cm**
- ☐ **1.35 m contrasting bias binding**

1   For the dark print placemat we outline-stitched the pattern with gold thread. To do this, baste wadding on wrong side of centre panel. Stitch outline through all thicknesses. Place wadding and centre panel onto wrong side of placemat, leaving border free.

For blue print placemat make up centre panel by stitching contrast strips together. Press. Place wadding onto wrong side of placemat. Place centre panel into place over wadding and baste through all thicknesses.

2   Fold and cut corners as shown in diagram A. Stitch to mitre corners, stitching up to 1 cm from edge. Press seams open.

3   Fold corners to right side. Turn under 1 cm along raw edges. Place bias binding under folded edges. Stitch down through all thicknesses. Press.

Note: See diagram, page 58.

❖
TOILET ROLL HOLDER

- ☐ **two strips cotton fabric, each 90 cm x 14 cm**
- ☐ **strip iron-on interfacing 90 cm x 14 cm**
- ☐ **3.2 m of 1.5 cm wide lace**
- ☐ **1.3 m of 3 mm wide satin ribbon**
- ☐ **small wooden curtain ring**
- ☐ **craft glue**

1   Interface one fabric strip. Trim one end of both strips to a point.

2   Stitch two 60 cm rows of lace down centre of fabric strip, beginning at pointed end and with straight edges of lace meeting in centre. Stitch ribbon over straight edges of lace, covering join and finishing with a bow.

3   With raw edges matching, stitch lace, on right side, around all sides of lace-trimmed piece, pleating lace at point and corners for ease.

4   Place both fabric pieces together with right sides facing and raw edges even. Stitch, following previous stitching line, leaving straight end open for turning. Trim fabric at points and corners. Turn and press.

5   Turn under 1 cm on straight end. Handsew this end to wrong side, below point and even with corners.

6   Cut strip of fabric 12 cm x 3 cm for loop. Fold over double lengthways. Stitch long side. Turn and press. Topstitch length with four rows of stitching.

7   Wind ribbon around to cover curtain ring. Glue ends to secure. Fold loop around ring, concealing ends of ribbon beneath loop. Glue to secure. Handsew ends of loop to wrong side of holder, at point. Trim with small bow.

8   Stitch across holder halfway between handsewing and lower folded edge, dividing it into two compartments.

❖
APPLIQUED TOWELS

- ☐ **towel**
- ☐ **remnant cotton print fabric**
- ☐ **double-sided bonding fabric**

1   Cut exact shape of motif to be appliqued from bonding fabric. Baste to wrong side of cotton fabric. Cut around motif, leaving 6 mm seam allowance.

2   Baste applique to towel. Iron into place.

3   Stitch around motif, 6 mm from edge, with narrow zigzag stitch. Trim away any excess fabric. Stitch around applique with a slightly wider satin stitch, covering previous stitching and raw edges.

Note: See motif patterns, pages 58-59.

A PPLIQUE T IPS

Choose pure cotton, silk or linen fabrics for the motif. Synthetics will be slippery and difficult to handle. If all cotton fabrics are chosen, use a pure cotton sewing thread to eliminate damage from high-temperature ironing.

PLACEMAT WITH SHAPED CORNERS

- ☐ **two pieces fabric 47 cm x 33 cm**
- ☐ **piece wadding 47 cm x 33 cm**
- ☐ **fabric scraps in three colours for applique**

1   Trim triangles evenly away from corners of wadding and fabric. Baste wadding to wrong side of one fabric piece.

2   Cut applique motif out of fabric scraps. Applique design onto fabric piece with wadding, following instructions given for towels.

3   Place both placemat pieces together with right sides facing. Stitch around outside edge, leaving opening for turning. Clip corners. Turn and press.

4   Stitch with a double row of stitches around shape of placemat and again 2 cm away.

Note: See diagram below.

TABLE NAPKIN WITH CONTRAST BORDER

- ☐ **square firm cotton fabric 47 cm x 47 cm**
- ☐ **four strips contrasting fabric 47 cm x 7 cm**
- ☐ **four strips second contrasting fabric 3 cm x 47 cm. You can use purchased piping or bias binding.**

1   Turn in 1 cm along one edge of each contrast border strip. Press.

2   Stitch adjoining strips together to form square, mitreing corners as shown in diagrams A and B. Press.

3   Place border and square together so that right side of border faces wrong side of square. Stitch together around outside edge. Trim corners, turn and press.

4   Place piping under inner edge of border. Stitch edge into place, through all thicknesses.

Note: See diagrams below.

TABLE NAPKIN WITH EMBROIDERED TRIM

- ☐ **56 cm square firm cotton fabric**
- ☐ **contrasting thread for embroidery**

1   Cut away corners of fabric as shown in diagram C.

2   Fold and stitch up to 1 cm from end as shown. Turn and press.

3   Turn under 1 cm around raw edges. Press. Stitch using a decorative machine stitch. See diagram D.

Note: See diagrams below.

Pretty table napkins and placemats with contrast centres

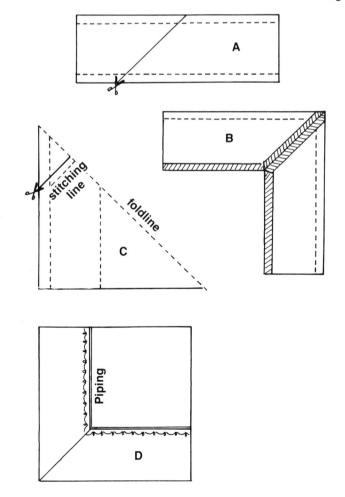

APPLIQUE BOWS

PLACE MAT APPLIQUE

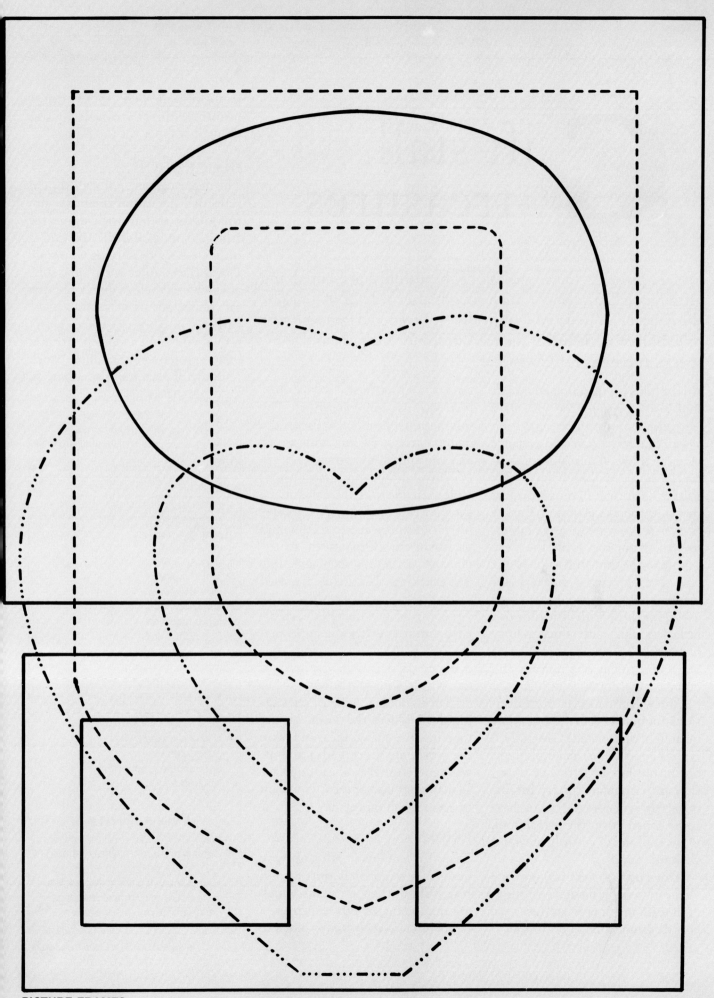

PICTURE FRAMES

Gift stall treasures

Perfect presents for all occasions, beautifully presented and giftwrapped, are always much sought after at fetes. Alongside the delicate knitted and beautifully embroidered items be sure to include a raffle prize, such as our lovely cushion, and some special treasures for Christmas.

All the hints for planning your craft stall also apply to the gift stall. Organise your team meeting as soon as you can. It will give you a chance to get to know your team and their special skills. Willing helpers may need assistance in finding a project that suits their level of skill. Ensure that there is a wide variety of items to make, ranging from the very simple to the quite difficult. Never turn away a willing worker! Remember that joint projects are very useful for those with little time or a little less skill. Introduce a busy sewer to someone who can't sew but who can cut out patterns and you have a productive little unit.

You will also need to make decisions about materials – should they be bought or donated? Generally, it is not a good idea to make gift items out of old bits of leftovers, unless they are particularly pretty. Buying materials will allow you to have some control over the overall look of the stall and to co-ordinate items with one another.

Draw up a master plan, showing all the items to be made. Give one to each team member with their own contribution highlighted. Organise copies of pattern, with clear instructions for everyone. The instructions should also list all the materials required, including trims, and any special wrappings.

There should be a clear timetable available to all team members, showing expected completion dates for various projects, collection and packaging days. Organise the schedule so that there is sufficient time for checking that items are well made and neatly finished. The wrapping of gift items is particularly important. Choose appropriate 'see-through' wrappings and decorate as extravagantly as you like with coloured ribbons.

Setting aside sewing or packaging days, where the team can get together to exchange ideas and share the work, are a great idea and always good fun. Plan ahead and have a fairly clear idea of what you want to accomplish on the day.

PRICES

Beautiful handmade gifts are very popular and can fetch quite a good price. Often they are items which are impossible to buy except at a fete or bazaars, such as embroidered, hand-knitted bed socks for a favourite Aunt or a truly decorative draught stopper for the home.

DECORATION

The decor of your gift stall should reflect all the fun of the fair – aim for lots of colour with drapes of fabric, clouds of balloons and a bright banner identifying your stall. Cover the counter with some suitable material before displaying the gift items, attractively laid out or gathered into pretty baskets. Don't crowd your stall and keep extras at hand to top up your counter. Stock a supply of plastic or paper bags to hold purchases.

ABBREVIATIONS
KNITTING AND CROCHET

K = Knit
P = Purl
st st = stocking stitch
rep = repeat
rem = remain
inc = increase
dec = decrease
patt = pattern
foll = following
alt = alternate
tog = together
rs = right side
ws = wrong side
kways = knitways
pways = purlways
yfwd = yarn forward
ybk = yarn back
psso = pass slipped stitch over
sl st = slip stitch
ch = chain
dc = double crochet
tr = treble

YARN GUIDE

We have chosen Cleckheaton yarns in this book, however, should they not be available to you, select your yarns in the ply specified. We have noted both metric and imperial needle sizes in our patterns.

A selection of gift stall treasures

❖
BED SOCKS

To fit average foot

MATERIALS

Cleckheaton 8 Ply Machine Wash (50 g) 3 balls; 1 pair 4 mm (No. 8) knitting needles and a spare 4 mm (No. 8) knitting needle.

TENSION

22 sts to 10 cm over st st, using 4 mm needles.

Using 4 mm needles, cast on 46 sts.
1st row: K2, *P2, K2, rep from * to end.
2nd row: P2, *K2, P2, rep from * to end.
Rep 1st and 2nd rows until rib measures 16 cm from beg, ending with a 2nd row and inc one st at each end of last row. 48 sts.
Proceed as follows:
Note: When turning, bring yarn to front of work, slip next st onto right hand needle, ybk, slip st back onto left hand needle, then turn and proceed as instructed. This avoids holes in work.
1st row: K32, turn.
2nd row: K16, turn.
Work 50 rows in garter st (every row K) on these 16 sts. Break off yarn.
With right side facing, join yarn to sts left on right hand needle and knit up 27 sts from side of instep, then knit up 8 sts across top of instep (toe sts).
Using another needle, knit rem 8 sts across top of instep (toe sts), knit up 27 sts from other side of instep, then knit across rem sts. 102 sts.
Work 17 rows garter st.
Next row: K1, K2tog, K46, (K2tog) twice, K46, K2tog, K1. 98 sts. Cont in this manner, dec at each end of both needles in every row until 86 sts rem. Cast off.

TO MAKE UP

Using a flat seam, join foot and leg seams, reversing seam for half of rib if desired. Fold rib onto right side.

❖
COAT HANGER COVER

To fit standard wooden coat hanger

MATERIALS

Cleckheaton 5 Ply Machine Wash (50 g): 1 ball for each hanger; 1 pair 3.75 mm (No. 9) knitting needles; wooden coat hanger; wadding; craft glue and plastic tubing (if desired); ribbon and flowers (or accessories as desired).

TENSION

26 sts to 10 cm over st st, using 3.75 mm needles.

Using 3.75 mm needles, cast on 18 sts.
Work 4 rows st st (1 row K, 1 row P).
Work 6 rows garter st (every row knit).
**11th row: K1, inc once in each of next 16 sts, K1. 34 sts.
Work 7 rows st st, beg with a purl row.
19th row: K1, (K2tog) 16 times, K1. 18 sts.
Work 5 rows garter st.**
Rep from ** to ** until work measures approx 20 cm from beg, ending with a 19th patt row.
Work 3 rows garter st.
Tie a coloured thread at each end of last row to denote centre.
Work 2 rows garter st.
Rep from ** to ** until work measures approx 38.5 cm from beg, ending with 5 rows of garter st, and noting to have same number of 34 stitch sections as other side of centre.
Work 4 rows st st. Cast off loosely.

TO MAKE UP

Using back stitch, sew up long side and one short end of cover. Remove hook from hanger and cover wooden section with wadding, using stitching or craft glue to secure wadding. Insert hanger into cover and stitch other short end closed. Cover hook with plastic tubing, or wind length of yarn around hook, then secure hook in top hole. Decorate with ribbon and silk flowers as illustrated.

❖
TEA COSY

Fits medium teapot

MATERIALS

Cleckheaton 8 Ply Machine Wash (50 g): 2 balls; 1 pair of 4 mm (No. 8) knitting needles.

TENSION

22 sts to 10 cm over st st, using 4 mm needles.

SPECIAL ABBREVIATIONS

C2F — Slip next 2 sts onto a cable needle and leave at front of work, K2, then K2 from cable needle.
C2B — Slip next 2 sts onto a cable needle and leave at back of work, K2, then K2 from cable needle.
C4F — Slip next st onto a cable needle and leave at front of work, K3, then K1 from cable needle.
C4B — Slip next 3 sts onto a cable needle and leave at back of work, K1, then K3 from cable needle.

First Piece
Using 4 mm needles, cast on 56 sts.
Knit 5 rows.
Commence pattern as follows:
1st row: P3, K4, P3, K9, P3, K4, P4, K4, P3, K9, P3, K4, P3.
2nd row: K3, P4, K3, P9, K3, P4, K4, P4, K3, P9, K3, P4, K3.
3rd row: P3, C2F, P3, C4F, K1, C4B, P3, C2B, P4, C2F, P3, C4f, K1, C4B, P3, C2B, P3.
4th row: K3, P4, K3, P9, K3, P4, K4, P4, K3, P9, K3, P4, K3.
Row 1 to 4 inclusive form patt.
Work 24 rows patt.
Shape top
Keeping patt correct, Next row: P2togtbl, patt 25, K2tog, patt to last 2 sts, P2tog.
Work 1 row.
Cont to dec in centre and at each end of next and every foll alt row until 29 sts rem.
Work 1 row.
Next row: K1, *K2tog, rep from * to end.
Draw yarn through rem sts and fasten off securely.

TO MAKE UP

Using a flat seam, join side seams leaving openings for spout and handle. Make twisted cords. Stitch to form loops on top.

KNITTING TIP

❖ Lightly pack bed socks with polyester fibre to fill them out to a foot shape. Then bundle them into clear cellophane tied with a bow.

❖ Place cardboard cut into the profile shape of your tea-pot into the tea cosy before wrapping.

❖ Cutting wadding into strips and winding these around the coathanger prior to covering will eliminate a lot of hand-stitching. Simply stitch ends to secure.

For the keen knitters, bed socks, coat hangers and tea cosy

❖
BABY'S MATINEE JACKET AND BONNET

To fit underarm	36	41	46 cm
Actual measurement	41	46	51 cm
Length to back neck (approximate)		25	30	33 cm
Sleeve seam (approximate)		12	13.5	16 cm

A new baby layette features matinee jacket, bonnet, singlet and bootees

MATERIALS

Cleckheaton Babysoft 3 Ply (25 g): 3 (4, 4) balls for jacket and 1 ball for bonnet; 1 pair each 3 mm (No. 11) and 2.75 mm (No. 12) knitting needles; 5 stitch holders; 4 buttons for jacket; 70 cm of 11 mm wide ribbon for bonnet.

TENSION

32 sts to 10 cm over st st, using 3 mm needles and 2 patts to 5.5 cm in width, using 3 mm needles.

JACKET (worked in one piece to underarm)

Using 3 mm needles, cast on 191 (207, 223) sts.

Work 8 rows garter st (every row K, 1st row is wrong side).

Next row: K6, slip these 6 sts onto length of yarn and leave, knit to last 6 sts, turn, leave rem 6 sts on length of yarn. 179 (195, 211) sts.

Beg patt:

1st row: K1, K2tog, *yfwd, K5, yfwd, sl 1, K2tog, psso, rep from * to last 8 sts, yfwd, K5, yfwd, sl 1, K1, psso, K1.

2nd and alt rows: Purl.

3rd row: As 1st row.

5th row: K3, *yfwd, sl 1, K1, psso, K1, K2tog, yfwd, K3, rep from * to end.

7th row: K1, K2tog, yfwd, K1, *yfwd, sl 1, K2tog, psso, yfwd, K1, rep from * to last 3

sts, yfwd, sl 1, K1, psso, K1.

8th row: As 2nd row.

Rows 1 to 8 inclusive form patt.

Cont in patt, until work measures approx 11.5 (16, 18.5) cm from beg, ending with an 8th patt row.

Divide for right front

1st row: Patt 45 (49, 53), turn.

Cont on these sts and work a further 22 (24, 26) rows patt.

Next row: P4 (2, 5), (P2tog) 18 (22, 22) times, P5 (3, 4). 27 (27, 31) sts.

Break off yarn, leave sts on a stitch holder. With right side facing, join yarn to next 89 (98, 105) sts for Back.

Work 23 (25, 27) rows patt.

Next row: P7, (P2tog) 37 (41, 45) times, P8. 52 (56, 60) sts.

Break off yarn, leave sts on a stitch holder. With right side facing, join yarn to rem sts and work Left Front to correspond with Right Front.

Sleeves

Using 2.75 mm needles, cast on 32 (37, 37) sts.

Work 6 rows garter st (1st row is wrong side).

Next row: K6 (7, 7), inc once in each of next 19 (22, 22) sts, K7 (8, 8). 51 (59, 59) sts.

Change to 3 mm needles.

Work in patt as for Jacket until work measures approx 12 (13.5, 16) cm from beg, ending with an 8th patt row.

Tie a coloured thread at each end of last row.

Work 23 (25, 27) rows patt.

Next row: P3 (1, 1), (P2tog, P1) 15 (19, 19) times, P3 (1, 1). 36 (40, 40) sts.

Break off yarn, leave sts on a stitch holder.

Yoke

With wrong side facing, slip sts from stitch holders onto a 3 mm needle in foll order, Left Front, 1st Sleeve, Back, 2nd Sleeve, then Right Front. 178 (190, 202) sts.

1st row; K1, K2tog, *K2, K2tog, rep from * to last 3 sts, K1, K2tog. 133 (142, 151) sts. Knit 1 row.

3rd row: K5 (4, 3), (K2tog, K9) 11 (12, 13) times, K2tog, knit to end. 121 (129, 137) sts.

Knit 3 rows.

7th row: K5 (4, 3), (K2tog, K8) 11 (12, 13) times, K2tog, knit to end. 109 (116, 123) sts.

Knit 3 rows.

11th row: K4 (3, 2), (K2tog, K7) 11 (12, 13) times, K2tog, knit to end. 97 (103, 109) sts. Knit 3 rows.

15th row: K4 (3, 2), (K2tog, K6) 11 (12, 13) times, K2tog, knit to end. 85 (90, 95) sts. Knit 3 rows.

19th row: K3 (2, 1), (K2tog, K5) 11 (12, 13) times, K2tog, knit to end. 73 (77, 81) sts. Knit 3 rows.

23rd row: K3 (2, 1), (K2tog, K4) 11 (12, 13) times, K2tog, K2 (1, 0). 61 (64, 67) sts. Knit 1 row. Break off yarn.

Leave sts on stitch holder.

Left Front Band

Slip 6 sts from thread onto a 2.75 mm needle. Join yarn to inside edge, inc in first st, knit to end.

Cont in garter st, until band is long enough to fit (slightly stretched) along front edge to top of yoke, working last row on wrong side.

Right Front Band

Work as for Left Front Band until there are 24 rows less.

**Next row: K3, cast off 2 sts, K2.

Next row: K2, cast on 2 sts, K3.

Knit 8 rows.**

Rep from ** to ** once, then buttonhole rows once. 3 buttonholes.

Knit 3 rows.

Leave sts on needle. Do not break off yarn.

Neckband

Using a 2.75 mm needle holding Right Front Band sts, knit across sts from stitch holder, then knit across sts from Left Front Band. 75 (78, 81) sts.

Knit 4 rows garter st, working a buttonhole (as before) in 2nd and 3rd rows. Cast off.

TO MAKE UP

Using back stitch, join sleeve seams to coloured threads, then join rem seam to body. Sew front bands in position. Sew on buttons.

BONNET

Using 3 mm needles, cast on 75 (83, 91) sts.

Work 5 rows garter st (1st row is wrong side).

Work 39 (47, 55) rows patt as for Jacket.

1st and 3rd Sizes Only — dec (inc) one st at each end of last row. 73 (83, 93) sts. Shape crown.

1st row: K9 (11, 17), (K2tog, K10) 5 (6, 5) times, (K2tog) 2 (0, 0) times, K0 (0, 16). 66 (77, 88) sts.

2nd and alt rows: Knit.

3rd row: (K2tog, K9) 6 (7, 8) times. 60 (70, 80) sts.

5th row: (K2tog, K8) 6 (7, 8) times. 54 (63, 72) sts.

7th row: (K2tog, K7) 5 (7, 8) times. 48 (56, 64) sts.

Cont dec in this manner in alt rows until 12 (14, 16) sts rem.

Break off yarn. Run end through rem sts, draw up and fasten off securely.

TO MAKE UP

Using a flat seam, join seam beg 2.5 cm from crown. Attach ribbon to each side of bonnet.

❖ BOOTEES

To fit 0-6 months

Note: For slightly smaller bootees use one size smaller needles than those which give correct tension. For slightly larger bootees use one size larger needles than those which give correct tension.

MATERIALS

Cleckheaton Babysoft 3 Ply (25 g): 1 ball of white for Garter Stitch Bootees and 1 ball each of white (MC) and pink (C) for Bootees with Rib Ankle; 1 pair 3 mm (No. 11) needles; about 85 cm of 6 mm wide ribbon for each pair.

TENSION

32 sts to 10 cm over st st, using 3 mm needles.

GARTER STITCH BOOTEES

Using 3 mm needles, cast on 43 sts.

1st row: (K1, inc in next st, K18, inc in next st) twice, K1.

2nd and alt rows: Knit.

3rd row: (K1, inc in next st, K20, inc in next st) twice, K1.

5th row: (K1, inc in next st, K22, inc in next st) twice, K1.

7th row: (K1, inc in next st, K24, inc in next st) twice, K1.

9th row: (K1, inc in next st, K26, inc in next st) twice, K1.

11th row: (K1, inc in next st, K28, inc in next st) twice, K1.

12th row: K2tog, K63, K2tog. 65sts. ***

Work 10 rows st st (1 row K, 1 row P).

Shape instep.

Next row: K37, K2tog, turn.

Next row: Sl 1, K9, K2tog, turn.

Rep last row until 45 sts rem (17 sts on each side of instep).

Next row: K10, K2tog, then knit to end.

Next row: Purl. 44 sts.

Ankle

Next row: K1, *yfwd, K2tog, rep from * to last st, K1.

Next row: Purl, inc one st in centre. 45 sts.

Next row: K2, *P1, K1, rep from * to last st, K1.

Next row: K1, *P1, K1, rep from * to end.

Rep last 2 rows 3 times.

Using C, work 14 rows garter st (every row K). Cast off.

TO MAKE UP

Using a flat seam, join foot and back seam, reversing back seam above rib.

Thread ribbon through eyelet holes and tie in a bow. Fold ankle section above rib to right side.

BOOTEES WITH RIB ANKLE

Using 3 mm needles and MC, cast on 43 sts.

Work as for Garter Stitch Bootees to ***

Work 10 rows st st (1 row K, 1 row P).

Shape instep

Next row: K37 K2tog, turn.

Next row: Sl 1, K9, K2tog, turn.

Next row: Sl 1, K9, K2tog, turn.

Rep last 2 rows until 45 sts rem (17 sts on each side of instep).

Next row: Sl 1, K9, K2tog, K16.

Next row: Purl. 44 sts.

Ankle

Next row: K1, *yfwd, K2tog, rep from * to last st, K1.

Using C, Next row: Purl, inc one st at each end. 46 sts.

Next row: K2, *P2, K2, rep from * to end.

Next row: P2, *K2, P2, rep from * to end.

Rep last 2 rows until rib section measures 8 cm from beg, working last row on wrong side. Cast off.

TO MAKE UP

Using a flat seam, join foot and back seam, reversing back seam for 4 cm at ankle edge. Thread ribbon through eyelet holes and tie in a bow. Fold half rib section onto right side.

Fancy Fairisle Bootees

❖ BABY'S SINGLET

To fit underarm	41 cm
Length	24 cm

MATERIALS

Cleckheaton Babysoft 3 Ply (25 g) 2 balls; 1 pair each 3 mm (No. 11) and 2.25 mm (No. 13) knitting needles; 3mm (No. 10-11) crochet hook.

TENSION

32 sts to 10cm over st st, using 3 mm needles.

BACK AND FRONT: (both alike)

Using 2.25 mm needles, cast on 61 sts.

1st row: K2, *P1, K1, rep from * to last st, K1.

2nd row: K1, *P1, K1, rep from * to end.

Rep 1st and 2nd rows until work measures 3 cm from beg, ending with a 2nd row.

Change to 3 mm needles.

Work in st st (1 row K, 1 row P), until work measures 16 cm from beg, ending with a purl row.

Beg Pattern

1st row: P2, *K3, yfwd, sl 1, K2tog, psso, yfwd, K3, P3, rep from * to last 11 sts, K3, yfwd, sl 1, K2tog, psso, yfwd, K3, P2.

2nd row: K2, *P9, K3, rep from * to last 11 sts, P9, K2.

3rd row: P2, *K1, K2tog, yfwd, K3, yfwd, sl 1, K1, psso, K1, P3, rep from * to last 11 sts, K1, K2tog, yfwd, K3, yfwd, sl 1, K1, psso, K1, P2.

4th row: As 2nd row.

Rep rows 1 to 4 inclusive 3 times.

Shape neck

1st row: Patt 13, cast off 35 sts, patt 13.

Cont on last 13 sts until work measures approx 24 cm from beg, ending with a purl row. Cast off.

Join yarn to rem sts and work other side to correspond.

TO MAKE UP

Using back stitch, join shoulder and side seams to beg of patt. Using hook, work 1 row double crochet evenly around neck edge having a number of sts divisible by 6. Next round: 1ch *1dc in first dc, miss 2dc, 5tr in next dc, miss 2dc, rep from * to end, sl st in 1ch at beg. Fasten off. Work same edging around armholes.

❖
FAIRISLE BOOTEES

To fit 0-6 months

MATERIALS

1 ball main colour (MC) 5 ply yarn, small quantities of 4 contrasting colours (C1, C2, C3 and C4); 1 pair 3.75 mm (No. 9) knitting needles; 6 mm wide ribbon.

TENSION

26.5 sts to 10 cm over st st, using 3.75 mm needles.

(Beg at sole)
Cast on 31 sts.

1st row: (Inc in next st, K13, inc in next st) twice, K1.
2nd, 4th and 6th rows: Purl.
3rd row: (Inc in next st, K15, inc in next st) twice, K1.
5th row: (Inc in next st, K17, inc in next st) twice, K1.
7th row: (Inc in next st, K19, inc in next st) twice, K1.(47 sts).
8th row: Knit.
9th row: Purl.
10th row: K3 (inc in next st, K4) 8 times, inc in next st, K3. (56 sts).
Using C1, work 2 rows st st.
Using C2, 13th row: K2* keeping yarn at back of work, Sl 1 pways, K2, rep from * to end.
14th row: Purl.
Using C3, rep 13th and 14th rows once.
Using C1, rep 13th and 14th rows once.
Using MC, 19th row: K3, (K2 tog, K4) 8 times, K2 tog, K3. (47 sts).
20th row: Knit.
21st row: Purl.
22nd row: Knit.
Shape instep
23rd row: K28, Sl 1 kways, K1, psso, turn.
24th row: P10, P2 tog, turn.
25th row: K10, Sl 1 kways, K1, psso, turn.
Rep 24th & 25th rows 5 times, then 24th row once.
Next row: K to end (33 sts).
Proceed as follows:
1st row: Purl
2nd row: K1 * yfwd, K2 tog, rep from * to end.
3rd row: P1 * K1, P1, rep from * to end.
4th row: K1 * P1, K1, rep from * to end.
Rep 3rd and 4th rows 4 times.
Using C1, knit 3 rows (15th row).
16th row: K6 (inc in next st, K4) 4 times, inc in next st, K6.
17th row: K2 *, keeping yarn at back of work, Sl 1 pways, K2, rep from * to end.
18th row: Purl.
Using C2,19th row: K2 * keeping yarn at back of work, Sl 1 pways, K2, rep from * to end.
20th row: Purl.
Using C3, rep 19th and 20th rows.
Change to C1: K6, (K2 tog, K4) 4 times, K2 tog, K6. 33 sts.
Knit next 2 rows.
Cast off kways.

TO MAKE UP

Using back stitch, join back seam, reversing seam half way. Using flat seam, join foot seam. Fold ankle sections over to right side. Thread ribbon through eyelet holes.

❖
KNITTED BALL

About 14 cm diameter.

MATERIALS:

Cleckheaton 8 Ply Machine Wash (50 g): 1 ball of white (MC) and 1 ball each of purple (C1) pale purple (C2), and pink (C3); 1 pair of 5.50 mm (No. 5) knitting needles; polyester fibre for filling.

TENSION:

15 sts to 10 cm over garter st, using 5.50 mm needles and yarn doubled.
Note: Yarn is used doubled throughout.

First Section
Using 5.50 mm needles and MC, cast on 24 sts.
Knit one row.
Next row: Knit to last 4 sts, turn.
Rep last row once.
Next row: Knit to last 8 sts, turn.
Rep last row once.
Next row: Knit to end.
Rep last row once.
Cast off loosely.
Work 2 more sections in MC, then 3 each in C1, C2 and C3.

TO MAKE UP

Using back stitch, join sections together as illustrated. Draw thread through edge sts at one end and gather tightly. Fasten off securely. Fill firmly, then draw thread through sts at other end. Gather and fasten off securely.

Knitted Ball

Dancing Dumpty ballerina and Knitted Ball

❖

DANCING DUMPTY

Height (excluding legs): about 19 cm.

MATERIALS

Cleckheaton 12 Ply Machine Wash (50 g): 1 ball of white (MC) and 1 ball each of blue (C1), pink (C2) and yellow (C3); 1 pair of 5.50 mm knitting needles; polyester fibre for filling; 14 cm of tape for attaching hair; scraps red, black and pink felt for decorating face; scrap black yarn for mouth; 42 cm of gathered lace for skirt; 100 cm of 6 mm wide pink ribbon (for shoes); 90 cm of 6 mm wide purple ribbon for hair and bow.

TENSION

17 sts to 10 cm over st st, using 5.50 mm needles.

Body (beg at lower edge)
Using MC cast on 6 sts.
1st row: Inc in each st to end. 12 sts.
2nd row: Purl.
3rd row: As 1st row. 24 sts.
Work 3 rows st st (1 row K, 1 row P), beg with a purl row.
7th row: As 1st row. 48 sts.
Work 7 rows, inc one st at each end of 1st row. 50 sts.

Using C1, work 6 rows.
Using MC, work 6 rows.
Next row: K6, *K2tog, K10, rep from * to last 8 sts, K2tog, K6. 46 sts.
Work 9 rows.
Next row: K5, *K2tog, K9, rep from * to last 8 sts, K2tog, K6. 42 sts.
Work 3 rows.
Next row: K2, *K2tog, K2, rep from * to end. 32 sts.
Next row: Purl.
Next row: K2, *K2tog, K1, rep from * to end. 22 sts.
Next row: Purl.
Next row: K1, (K2tog) 10 times, K1. 21 sts.
Next row: Purl.
Next row: (K2tog) 6 times. 6 sts.
Break off yarn, run end through rem sts, draw up and fasten off securely.

Arms (make 2 – beg at top)
Using C1, cast on 12 sts.
Work 4 rows st st.
Using MC, work 10 rows st st.
Next row: (K2tog) 6 times. 6 sts.
Break off yarn, run end through rem sts, draw up and fasten off securely.

Legs (make 2 — beg at top)
Using MC, cast on 14 sts.
Work 18 rows st st.

Using C2, work 8 rows.
Next row: (K2tog) 7 times. 7 sts.
Break off yarn, run end through rem sts, draw up and fasten off securely.

TO MAKE UP

Using back stitch, join body seam, leaving an opening for stuffing, and drawing 6 'cast-on' sts together. Stuff firmly and sew up opening.

Join arm and leg seams, leaving top edges open for stuffing. Stuff firmly and oversew 'cast-on' edges.

Stitch arms to middle body stripe at sides, and stitch legs to body 2 rows up from last dec at beg.

Cut eyes, nose and cheeks from felt and sew into position. Embroider mouth using stem stitch. Stitch lace around body at first row of C1.

To make hair sew a few loops of yarn to forehead as pictured.

Cut rest of C3 into 50 cm lengths. Cut a 14 cm length of tape and stitch centre of lengths evenly along tape, leaving 1 cm of tape free at each end.

Turn under ends of tape. Stitch hair (through tape) to head as illustrated. Trim ends and tie into bunches using purple ribbon. Tie a purple bow to front. Tie pink ribbon around legs as shown.

❖
RAFFLE CUSHION

- ☐ piece white hardanger 50 cm x 50 cm with 22 threads to 2.5 cm
- ☐ stranded embroidery cotton in colours indicated
- ☐ two pieces firm cotton fabric for cushion back, each 23 cm x 42 cm
- ☐ 3.2 m of 10 cm wide lace
- ☐ 40 cm x 40 cm lightweight, white cotton for backing embroidered panel
- ☐ 40 cm x 40 cm cushion insert
- ☐ 30 cm zipper

1   Embroider hardanger panel following Embroidery graph and Stitch guide.
2   Place embroidered panel on white backing. Baste together around edges.
3   Join ends of centre back seam of cushion in 1 cm seam, leaving centre 30 cm open for zipper. Insert zipper.
4   Gather lace to 162 cm. Pin and baste lace around embroidered panel, matching raw edges.
5   Place cushion back and front together with right sides facing. Stitch around edges through all thicknesses. Turn to right side through zipper opening.

A rose embroidered cushion makes a popular raffle prize.

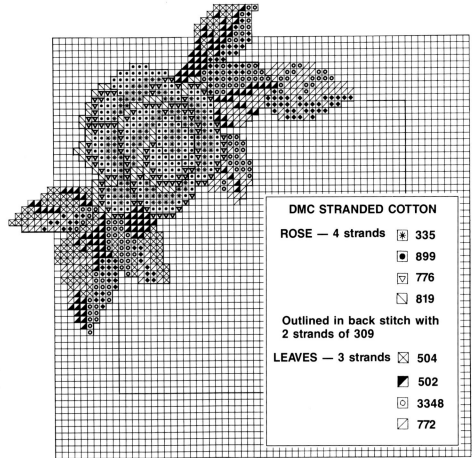

DMC STRANDED COTTON

ROSE — 4 strands ⊛ 335

⬤ 899

▽ 776

◹ 819

Outlined in back stitch with 2 strands of 309

LEAVES — 3 strands ⊠ 504

◩ 502

⊙ 3348

⧄ 772

❖ DRAUGHT STOPPERS

- ☐ **strip of velvet 22 cm x 115 cm**
- ☐ **embroidery thread for grub roses**
- ☐ **strong ribbon or braid for tying ends**
- ☐ **clean sand for filling**

1   Embroider an oval of grub roses onto centre of velvet and 25 cm from each end, following instructions in How to embroider grub roses.

2   Fold velvet so that long sides are even and right sides are facing. Stitch long side in 1 cm seam. Turn.

3   Fold in 10 cm at one end. Tie off very securely about 8 cm from end. Fill with sand, using a funnel. Shake frequently to settle sand. When tube is filled fold in 10 cm at open end and tie off securely as before.

HOW TO EMBROIDER
GRUB ROSES

Grub roses are stitched in toning shades of stranded cotton, starting with darkest shade at centre and working out to lightest shade. Stitch leaves in bullion knots or chain stitch in tones of green.

Bring needle up at A. Take a stitch from B to A; do not pull needle through (A to B equals the width of knot required). Twist thread several times around needle clockwise covering width of AB. Pull needle through easing twisted thread onto fabric. Re-insert needle at B. Build up bullion knots as shown below.

Grub rose layout diagram

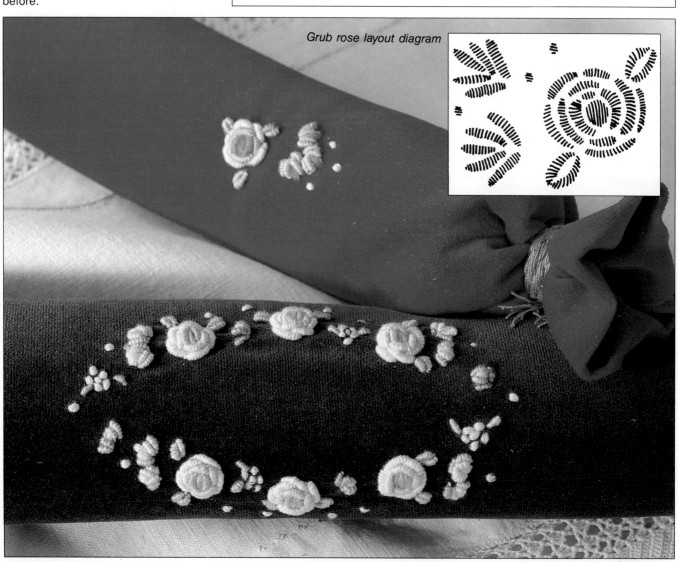

The ultimate draught stoppers embroidered with grub roses

❖
HOT WATER BOTTLE COVER

- ☐ **two pieces open-weave, soft wool fabric, each 40 cm x 29 cm**
- ☐ **60 cm of 3 cm wide cotton lace**
- ☐ **1 m of 12 mm wide satin ribbon**
- ☐ **yarn for embroidery**

1   Round off lower corners of both pieces of fabric. Embroider flowers and leaves onto front of one fabric piece as shown.

2   Place fabric pieces together with right sides facing. Stitch both long sides and one short end in 1 cm seam, leaving 8 cm open in sewn short end. Turn to right side.

3   Sew around opening in sewn end, using blanket stitch and toning yarn, securing seam allowance as you go.

4   Stitch lace around open end. Thread ribbon through fabric, approximately 10 cm from lace-trimmed edge and tie into bow. If easier, make small buttonholes.

Grub roses embroidered on hot water bottle cover

E MBROIDERY T IP

Grub roses are delightful, traditional embroidery motifs for the most feminine, personal and household items. You will require patience, and a little resolve, as the positioning of the 'grubs' determines the shape of your rose. Build up the stitches – placing some on top of others to give the rose depth and texture. Experts like to use five or six strands of thread when sewing, but experiment for yourself. The thicker the thread, the larger the rose, so try working in wool yarn instead of stranded cotton. Remember, the first rose is by far the hardest to make!

Detail of hot water bottle cover embroidery

❖
MOUSE IN A BALLOON

BALLOON
- [ ] **15 cm polystyrene foam ball**
- [ ] **six 30 cm x 10 cm strips fabric in two or three co-ordinating prints**
- [ ] **three 50 cm lengths of 2 cm wide insertion lace**
- [ ] **3.5 m of 6 mm wide satin ribbon**
- [ ] **1 m gathered lace**
- [ ] **small cane basket**
- [ ] **scrap fabric to line basket**

MOUSE
- [ ] **squares white and scraps pink and black felt**
- [ ] **polyester fibre for stuffing**
- [ ] **30 cm x 8 cm strip fabric for dress**
- [ ] **30 cm length broderie anglaise or wide lace for petticoat**
- [ ] **30 cm gathered lace**

EQUIPMENT
- [ ] **three large elastic bands**
- [ ] **Stanley knife or sharp-pointed knife**
- [ ] **metal nail file**

BALLOON

1   Divide foam ball into six equal segments using elastic bands. It is best to lift and place bands into place rather than rolling them. When you are certain all segments are exactly equal, mark divisions with a fine pencil line.

2   With Stanley knife blade extended to about 12 mm and using a sawing action, cut along pencil lines, making sure they intersect at top and bottom of ball.

3   Cut six pieces of fabric to approximate size and shape of segments with 6 mm allowance all around. Pin each piece into place and, with a metal nail file, poke excess fabric carefully all the way into grooves already cut. Repeat until ball is covered.

4   Cut three lengths of insertion lace to go around ball through top and bottom points of intersection. Thread two 70 cm and one 75 cm length of ribbon into insertion lace, leaving approximately 21 cm of ribbon extending from one end of lace. These will attach to basket.

5   Measure 9 cm up every second line from intersection of lines on bottom of ball. Mark with a pencil. Beginning at one pencil mark, glue insertion lace with 70 cm ribbon down to bottom of ball and around to pencil mark again. Do not overlap lace at join. Repeat for other 70 cm length. When glueing lace with 75 cm length of ribbon, draw out 5 cm of ribbon at point of ball to form loop for hanging.

6   Mark 9 cm up from bottom along other three lines. These mark top of scallops of gathered lace. Draw in scalloped line with pencil to ensure it is even all around. Glue gathered lace along this line, making curves and points very pronounced and having lace join at one point. Glue bows to each point of scallops, covering join.

7   Glue free ends of ribbon, evenly spaced, around lip of small basket, taking care that basket hangs as straight as possible. It may be helpful to hold ribbons into place with pegs until glue dries.

8   Neaten raw edge of fabric scrap and handsew it inside basket. Decorate basket with lace and bows as shown.

MOUSE

1   Cut out one body piece. Fold double along foldline. Stitch seam, leaving base open. Trim seam and turn. Stuff firmly.

2   Run gathering thread around base. Pull up tightly and secure to close.

3   Embroider eyes and nose with satin stitch, taking threads from one to the other through head.

4   Glue pink inner ear to white outer ear with lower edges even. Fold ears in half at lower edge. Cut slits for ears in sides of head. Glue ears into slits.

5   Glue two foot pieces together for added stability. Glue on feet and tail.

6   To dress girl mouse, fold arms over double lengthways and glue to fix. Glue arms around body, approximately 1 cm below ears.

7   Press in 1 cm hem on top and lower edges of fabric strip for dress. Stitch lace around lower edge. Place top edge of petticoat under fold of top edge of dress. Gather top edge of dress and petticoat at same time. Cut slits for arms in dress and petticoat. Thread arms through. Shape hands. Tie bow on tail.

8   To dress boy mouse, glue on waistcoat with small amount of glue. Make arms as for girl and glue sleeves around them. Trim arms and shape hands. Fold and glue collar into place. Glue coat to mouse. Glue arms to mouse. Finish with bow tie, pearl stud and bow for tail.

Dainty lace and ribboned balloon with fashionably dressed mice

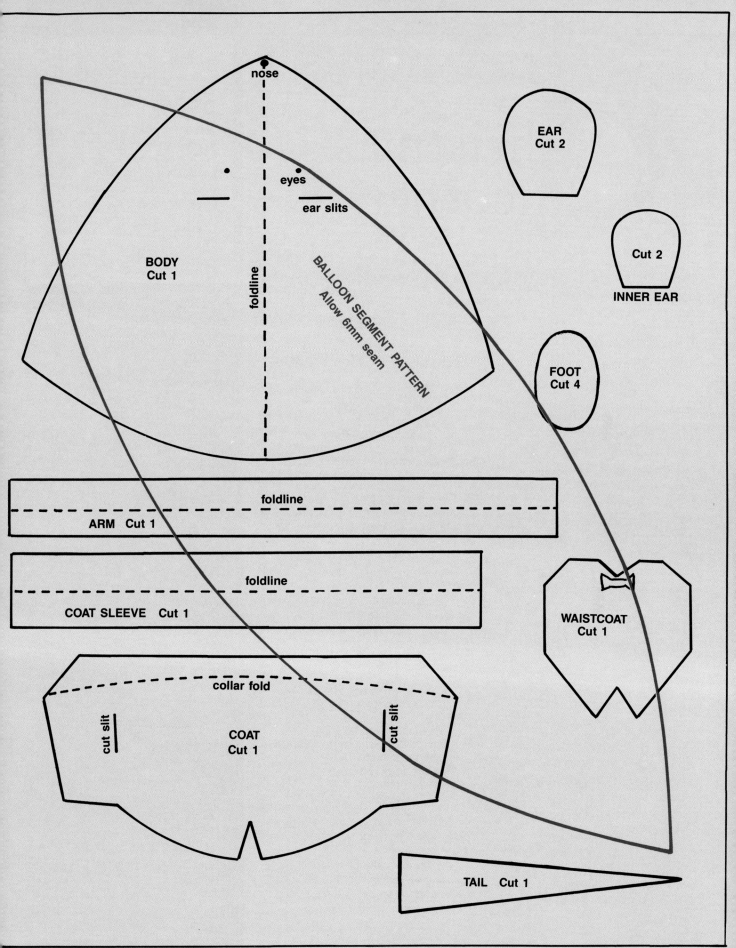

nose

eyes

ear slits

BODY
Cut 1

foldline

BALLOON SEGMENT PATTERN
Allow 6mm seam

EAR
Cut 2

Cut 2

INNER EAR

FOOT
Cut 4

foldline

ARM   Cut 1

foldline

COAT SLEEVE   Cut 1

WAISTCOAT
Cut 1

collar fold

cut slit

cut slit

COAT
Cut 1

TAIL   Cut 1

MOUSE IN A BALLOON

Christmas corner

So many fetes and bazaars are held in the festive season, they are the perfect place to pick up that unusual Christmas gift – or even better, pick up some great ideas for making your own!

We have plenty of ideas for decorating your home and office in truly traditional style around Christmas time.

Decorate your stall with examples of our Christmas wreath or, if you can, beg or borrow a small Christmas tree and use it to show off our easy-to-make bread dough ornaments and reindeer. Enlist the help of your children to search for well-shaped twigs to use for antlers on the reindeer.

Create an especially attractive presentation by using our cane basket with mixed nuts as a centrepiece. Get as large a basket as possible and decorate as festively as you like with plenty of red and green ribbon. Alternatively use several small baskets, as we have, and arrange them around the stall.

For gift ideas, we have included deliciously scented sachets in a variety of shapes, sizes and fabrics which can be trimmed in any way you like. People of all ages will love receiving their gifts in our Christmas stockings!

Don't forget how much everyone loves overeating around Christmas and give your family and friends a good excuse with our delicious mini puddings, chocolates and mixed nuts.

❖
CHRISTMAS CHOCOLATES

Makes about 25 squares

- ☐ **200 g mixed dried fruit**
- ☐ **400 g dark chocolate, melted**
- ☐ **40 g solid white coconut fat (copha) or vegetable shortening**
- ☐ **3 tablespoons brandy**
- ☐ **3 tablespoons chopped almonds**

1 Soak fruit in brandy overnight.
2 Melt coconut fat and chocolate separately. Combine them in a bowl. Stir in soaked fruit and nuts. If mixture is too moist, add some desiccated coconut.
3 Spread mixture into 26 cm x 18 cm shallow cake tin. Refrigerate until set for cutting into squares. For chocolate balls, roll mixture into balls when partially set.
4 Wrap chocolates individually in cellophane. Tie with ribbon.

❖
CANE BASKET WITH MIXED NUTS

- ☐ **cane basket with lid**
- ☐ **1.8 m of 2 cm wide tartan ribbon**
- ☐ **mixed nuts in shell**
- ☐ **clear-drying craft glue**
- ☐ **clear varnish**

1 Glue lengths of tartan ribbon to basket lid, from one side to the other, crossing at centre. Make loops of tartan ribbon and glue to centre of lid.
2 Varnish a variety of nuts with clear varnish. Allow to dry. Glue nuts around and between ribbon loops.
3 Fill basket with mixed nuts.

Christmas corner

Beautiful Christmas decorations

1 Break pudding into large chunks and place in bowl of food processor or blender. Add rum or brandy, coconut fat and jam. Process until just combined.
2 Shape mixture into balls to fit foil patty cases. Refrigerate until firm.
3 To make icing, beat egg white with lemon juice until frothy. Add icing sugar, a spoonful at a time. Beat well after each addition until icing just runs from spoon.
4 Trickle icing onto top of pudding and decorate with holly leaves and berries.

❖

CHRISTMAS STOCKINGS

- [ ] **exact fabric requirements will depend on the print you choose. Use 50 cm of 115 cm wide cotton of vertically striped fabric or 35 cm of 115 cm wide all-over print cotton.**
- [ ] **20 cm contrasting cotton or felt**
- [ ] **35 cm lightweight wadding**
- [ ] **braids, ribbon, lace, bells and holly for trimming**

1 Cut two stocking shapes each from main fabric and wadding. Cut two heels, two toes, two stocking tops. Cut two top facings from contrasting fabric or felt for fabric stockings. If using felt, scallop inner edges of contrast pieces by drawing around half shape of machine bobbin and cutting around outline.
2 Place wadding sections against wrong side of stocking pieces; baste. Baste contrast pieces into place, folding under any raw edges not covered by braid.
3 Stitch contrast pieces and any decorative braid into place. Scalloped felt pieces are stitched just inside scallops.
4 Place two stocking sections together with right sides facing. Stitch. Clip seams. Turn and press. For felt stockings, stitch around top again, trimming felt close to stitching.
5 For fabric stockings place top edge facings together with right sides facing. Stitch short ends. Place facing around stocking top with right sides together. Stitch around top edge. Turn facing to inside. Press. Neaten raw edge and handsew inside stocking.
6 Stitch loop of braid to heel side for hanging stocking.
7 Stitch your choice of Christmas trims into place, using our examples as a guide.

❖

CHRISTMAS WREATHS

- [ ] **wreath base purchased from florist or specialty shop**
- [ ] **variety of suitable trims such as holly leaves and berries, seed pods, nuts, artificial fruit, flowers and ribbons**
- [ ] **small loop wire for hanging**
- [ ] **spray paint, if desired**
- [ ] **hot melt glue gun or other suitable colourless craft glue**

1 Spray paint wreath and allow to dry before decorating.
2 Plan layout for decoration before you begin to glue.
3 Prepare all trims – tie bows, spray paint, nuts and gather small items into bunches.
4 Glue decorations into place.
5 Make a wire loop at centre back for hanging wreath.

❖

REINDEER

- [ ] **pieces wood about 3 cm thick and 5 cm long for head; 4 cm thick and 10 cm long for body; 1.5 cm thick and 7 cm long for neck; 1 cm thick and 3 cm long for tail**
- [ ] **twigs for antlers**
- [ ] **scraps leather or vinyl for ears**
- [ ] **four 10 cm lengths of 1 cm thick dowelling for legs**

- [ ] **holly, berries, gold cord and other suitable Christmas decorations**
- [ ] **craft glue or hot-melt glue gun**

1 Drill small holes for antlers on top of head. Glue antlers into place.
2 Cut out ear shapes. Glue into place under antlers.
3 Drill holes for legs. Position legs so that reindeer stands securely. Glue legs into place.
4 Glue head to neck. Glue neck to body.
5 Glue on tail at an angle.
6 Cut eyes out of white paper, paint in pupils. Glue on eyes.
7 Trim with Christmas decorations. Glue on cord for hanging.

❖

MINI CHRISTMAS PUDDINGS

Makes 6 mini puddings

- [ ] **400 g canned Christmas pudding**
- [ ] **2 tablespoons rum or brandy**
- [ ] **30 g coconut fat (copha) or vegetable shortening, melted**
- [ ] **foil patty cases**
- [ ] **2 tablespoons raspberry jam**

ICING
- [ ] **1 egg white**
- [ ] **1 or 2 drops lemon juice**
- [ ] **$1^1/_4$ cups pure icing sugar**

HEAVEN SCENT

We have included wonderful scented sachets in a variety of shapes and sizes. They can be made in any light-weight fabric and trimmed with narrow or wide ribbon bows and silk, artificial or dried flowers. Sachets may be filled in any number of ways – with potpourri, lavender, napthalene flakes or moth balls. A very simple and inexpensive filling is achieved by moistening a cotton wool ball with your choice of per-fumed oil and wrapping this in polyester fibre.

❖ CIRCULAR SCENTED BUNDLES

- ☐ **pieces pretty cotton print fabric, voile, lace or hessian in desired size**
- ☐ **lace and ribbon for trimming**
- ☐ **small wooden curtain ring for hanging (optional)**
- ☐ **3 mm wide satin ribbon**
- ☐ **artificial or dried flowers**
- ☐ **your choice of fillings: naptha-lene for moths, lavender or potpourri for sweet smells, or polyester fibre, enclosing a cotton ball saturated with a favourite scent or floral oil**

1   Cut circle of fabric in size you have chosen. Neaten edge with pinking shears, zigzag stitch or hem.
2   Sew small gathering thread 2 cm from edge. You can choose a narrower or wider frill by moving this gathering in or out. Draw up gathering slightly.
3   Fill bundle. Close by pulling up gathering tightly, tucking in flowers if desired. Tie threads to secure.
4   Tie bows around gathering and attach flowers.
5   Using buttonhole stitch, weave 3 mm ribbon around curtain ring until covered. Attach ring to bundle with length of ribbon.

❖ SACHETS

- ☐ **pieces fabric or lace 17 cm x 15 cm**
- ☐ **tulle for lining in same size**
- ☐ **lace to trim and ribbon for ties**
- ☐ **potpourri**

If sachet is to be embroidered, this must be done before sewing, using How To Embroider Grub Roses instructions and illustration of embroidery layout.
1   Fold fabric over double, with right sides together, to form sachets 8.5 cm wide. If lining is to be used place both fabrics together before stitching and treat as a single layer.
2   Stitch both sides. Turn and press.
3   If using fabric which is unfinished at top edge, turn in 6 mm and again 2 cm. Stitch. You can stitch narrow lace around top edge of sachet or wider lace around throat to decorate.
4   Fill to throat with potpourri. Tie ribbon around throat to secure.

❖ BONBONS

- ☐ **16 cm double-edged scalloped lace about 20 cm wide**
- ☐ **tulle for lining in same size**
- ☐ **ribbon for trimming**
- ☐ **potpourri or desired filling**

1   Sew raw edges of lace together to form tube. If lining is to be used, place both fabrics together before sewing and treat as single layer.
2   Tie bow around one end.
3   Fill with potpourri and tie bow around other end.

❖ TALCUM-FILLED RIBBONS

- ☐ **50 cm lengths of 4 cm wide fancy satin ribbon**
- ☐ **3 mm ribbon for trimming**
- ☐ **talcum powder (purchased or made yourself using following directions)**

1   To make talcum powder, combine in a bowl 3 parts cornflour to 1 part orrisroot to two teaspoons of your favourite floral oil. Mix well and store in an airtight jar for about a month, mixing occasionally.
2   Fold length of ribbon in half with wrong sides facing. Stitch sides.
3   Fold in ends. Fill with talcum powder. Tie bow around top to secure.

❖ DOILY SACHETS

- ☐ **small cotton lace doily**
- ☐ **tulle for lining**
- ☐ **narrow ribbon for trimming**
- ☐ **potpourri**

1   Baste doily and tulle together.
2   Sew around inner circle of doily, form-ing a pocket for potpourri and leaving a small opening for stuffing. Trim away excess tulle. Fill with potpourri, lavender or moth balls. Close opening by hand. If doily centre is a very open weave, line it with an extra layer of tulle as well as backing it with tulle. Fill between two layers of tulle.
3   Trim with bows and ribbons for hanging sachet, if desired.

Lovely scented sachets trimmed with bows and flowers

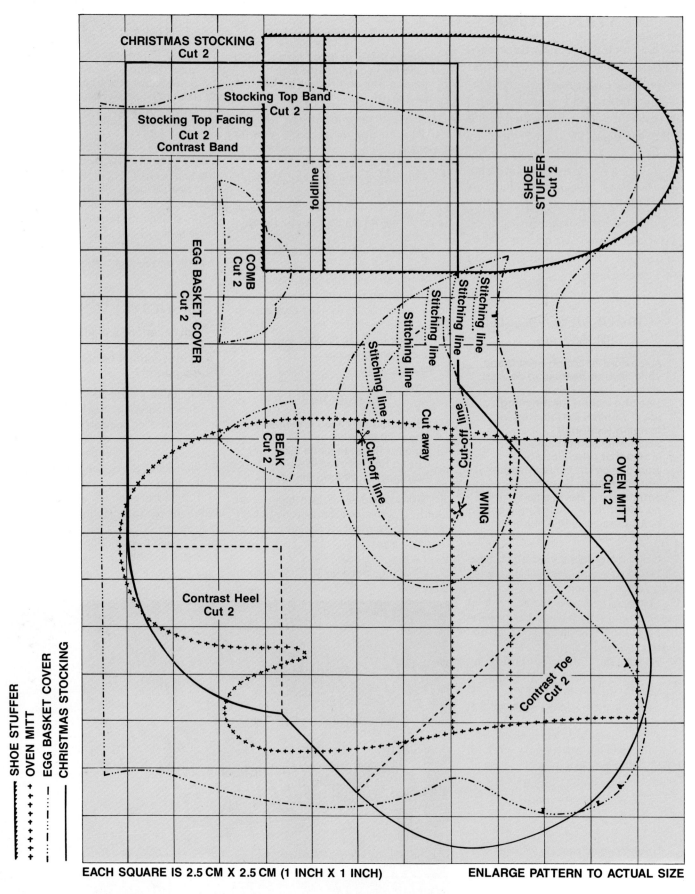

CHRISTMAS STOCKING
Cut 2

Stocking Top Band
Cut 2

Stocking Top Facing
Cut 2
Contrast Band

foldline

EGG BASKET COVER
Cut 2

COMB
Cut 2

SHOE
STUFFER
Cut 2

Stitching line
Stitching line
Stitching line
Stitching line

Cut away

Cut-off line

Cut-off line

BEAK
Cut 2

WING

OVEN MITT
Cut 2

Contrast Heel
Cut 2

Contrast Toe
Cut 2

SHOE STUFFER
OVEN MITT
EGG BASKET COVER
CHRISTMAS STOCKING

EACH SQUARE IS 2.5 CM X 2.5 CM (1 INCH X 1 INCH)   **ENLARGE PATTERN TO ACTUAL SIZE**

Glossary

Bicarbonate of Soda	Baking soda
Blood plums	Damson plums
Buttermilk	The liquid left from separated cream, slightly sour in taste
Copha	A white fat made from coconut oil, if unavailable use a white vegetable fat
Cornflour	Cornstarch, substitute arrowroot
Cream	Light pouring cream
Dark chocolate	Plain chocolate
Essence	Extract
Full spice powder	A mixture of ground spices which include cinnamon, cloves, fennel, star anise and Szechuan pepper
Garam masala	Made up of cardamon, cinnamon, cloves, coriander, cumin and nutmeg, often used in Indian cooking
Golden syrup	Honey can be substituted
Green capsicum	Green sweet pepper
Lemon butter	Lemon curd
Mixed fruit	A combination of sultanas, raisins, currants, mixed peel and cherries
Mixed spice	A finely ground combination of spices including caraway, allspice, coriander, cumin, nutmeg, ginger and cinnamon
Pork fillets	Skinless, boneless eye fillet
Rice flour	Substitute ground rice
Scone tray	Baking tray
Shallots	Spring onions
Weet-Bix	Weeta bix
White vinegar	Distilled malt vinegar
Zucchini	Courgette

MEASURING UP

Metric	Inches
2 mm	1/16
6 mm	1/4
1 cm	3/8
2.5 cm	1
5 cm	2
30 cm	12
91 cm	36

Cups	
1/4 cup	60 mL
1/3 cup	80 mL
1/2 cup	125 mL
1 cup	250 mL

Spoons	
1/4 teaspoon	1.25 mL
1/2 teaspoon	2.5 mL
1 teaspoon	5 mL
1 tablespoon	20 mL

For measuring ingredients in our recipes we have used a nest of metric measuring cups and a set of metric measuring spoons. All cup and spoon measures are level.

QUICK METRIC IMPERIAL CONVERTER

g	oz	mL	fl.oz
30	1	30	1
60	2	60	2
125	4	125	4
250	8	250	8
370	12	370	12
500	16	500	16

Index

ACKNOWLEDGEMENTS
The publishers would like to thank the following
for their assistance during recipe testing and
photography for this book: Admiral Appliances,
Blanco Appliances, Knebel Kitchens, Leigh Mardon
Pty Ltd, Master Foods of Australia, Meadow Lea
Foods, Namco Cookware, Sunbeam Corporation
Ltd, White Wings Foods; Mosmania of Mosman;
Accoutrement; Australian East India Company
Fabrics by Liberty
Ribbons by Offray
Wrapping paper supplied by Addarap; pot plants
supplied by Northcote Pottery Pty Ltd
All craft items sewn on Bernina and Pfaff sewing
machines; plants photographed at Michele
Shennen's Garden Centre, Sydney, Australia